Woodturning Traditional Folk Toys

Alan & Gill Bridgewater

STERLING PUBLISHING CO., INC.
NEW YORK

Dedication

When Alan was a kid, he received a set of wooden skittles for Christmas; our children played with tops and yo-yo's—we have all, at some time or other, played with woodturned traditional folk toys.

We would like to dedicate this book to all the anonymous toymakers of the past—all the cottage crafts men and women whose toys have given so much pleasure and joy to countless generations of children.

Acknowledgments

We would very much like to thank all the many individuals who helped us with this book:

Glen Tizzard—Draper Tools Ltd.—for the lathe and scroll saw.

John P. Jodkin—Vice President, Delta International—for the beautiful drill press.

Jim Brewer—Freud—for the Forstner drill bits.

Tracy Emmison—Humbrol paints.

And many others. Thank you.

Library of Congress Cataloging-in-Publication Data

Bridgewater, Alan.
    Woodturning traditional folk toys / Alan & Gill Bridgewater.
       p. cm.
  Includes index.
  ISBN 0-8069-8708-1
  1. Wooden toy making. 2. Turning. I. Bridgewater, Gill
  II. Title.
  TT174.5.W6B747   1994
  745.592—dc20   94-16756
                                     CIP

Edited by Rodman Neumann

10 9 8 7 6 5 4 3 2 1

Published by Sterling Publishing Company, Inc.
387 Park Avenue South, New York, N.Y. 10016
© 1994 by Alan & Gill Bridgewater
Distributed in Canada by Sterling Publishing
% Canadian Manda Group, One Atlantic Avenue, Suite 105
Toronto, Ontario, Canada M6K 3E7
Distributed in Great Britain and Europe by Cassell PLC
Villiers House, 41/47 Strand, London WC2N 5JE, England
Distributed in Australia by Capricorn Link (Australia) Pty Ltd.
P.O. Box 6651, Baulkham Hills, Business Centre, NSW 2153, Australia
Manufactured in the United States of America
All rights reserved

Sterling ISBN 0-8069-8708-1

Contents

Color section follows page 64.

Preface

Throughout the ages children have by nature engaged in play, thereby discovering their growing energy and stamina. At first they are happy enough just reaching out to their immediate surroundings—their own fingers and toes, and anything else they find nearby—but very soon, they yearn for objects to play with. In the dim and distant past, children made do with found natural items, such as sticks, nuts, stones, bones, shells, and feathers, and they shaped them according to their own skills and fancies. Gradually however, a time came when skilled parents and craftsmen created playthings for the child.

From a very early period, woodworking craftsmen, especially woodturners, spent some part of their working day making small toys, such as dolls, balls, skittles, and tops. According to old German engravings—one by Jost Amman dated A.D. 1568 and another by Christoff Weigel dated A.D. 1698—the woodturner had pride of place when it came to making toys. Old accounts suggest that when the village woodturner wasn't busy making run-of-the-mill domestic bowls, dishes, mugs, and such, then he was fully occupied making dolls, rattles, jumping jacks, spinning tops, and all manner of toys that were round or part-round in cross section. No doubt the turner used all of his off-cuts for the toys.

Czechoslovakia—Rocking baby doll. The arms pivot up and down—as if the swaddled baby is being rocked to sleep. Early twentieth century.

Czechoslovakia—Traditional churning doll toy. When the string is pulled, the figure goes up and down—as if she is churning butter. Probably made in the 1950s.

England—An early illustration showing children playing with spinning tops.

In the late sixteenth century the craze for playing cup-and-ball swept across France and the rest of Europe. (Detail taken from a contemporary print)

5

European, Germany, perhaps—A traditional pendulum toy. When the pendulum is swung, the woman works the churn and the cat laps up milk. Toys of this type were exported all over the world to be sold as Christmas stocking fillers. Early twentieth century.

Germany, Erzgebirge—Wooden soldiers and their barracks. Late nineteenth century.

England—A small turned double-cone diabolo toy. This child might actually have been too young to play this game, but it makes for a pretty picture. Nineteenth century.

The woodturner was at an advantage over the woodcarver or the general woodworker in that he was able to produce large numbers of almost identical forms, at speed, with a minimum of waste.

I think we all understand that woodturned toys are wooden toys that have been made on the lathe. But what do we mean by the phrase "traditional folk toys"?

Well, traditional folk toys are the common everyday toys that were/are made by cottage craftsmen. Certainly this definition can be filled out a bit with details, but how better can we describe, or put a name to, all the wooden toys that have been made for many hundreds of years by ordinary uncultured folk?

In the past, when children wanted a wooden toy, we either rolled up our sleeves and made it ourselves, or took a trip to the village woodturner and explained our needs—or, if we were lucky, we waited for the next peddler or hawker to pay us a visit.

Certainly we can all understand that there was a need for turned wooden toys, but how come no matter when and where the toys were made, they all seem to possess a wonderful naive sameness that marks them out as belonging to the folk tradition? Well, before TV, books, and magazines, before the industrial revolution, when woodworking skills were passed on one to one, and from village to village, when a cottage woodturner made a toy—in Germany, England, Poland, Sweden, the United States or wherever—he was not only making a doll or skittle to his own design, but also, in some small part, he was making a toy that related to hundreds of years of

Groden, German-speaking part of the South Tyrol—Acrobats pull-along toy. End of the nineteenth century.

Czechoslovakia, Krusnehory—A traditional "clatter" or "tinkle" toy. On some upmarket versions of this toy, the birds on the ground peck up and down—as if feeding—while the birds on the top of the house turn round.

custom and tradition. Or to put it in simple terms, the toy that he made was the direct result of the tools, the materials, the techniques, and his environment.

Of all the woodturned folk toy traditions, I think it fair to say that German folk toys have long been the most influential. As early as the fifteenth century Germany was known to be an international trading center. This is not to say that German toys are necessarily better, only that Germany's reputation as a producer of toys is founded on the activities of its merchants and exporters.

From a very early date, well-organized German cottage industries, cooperatives, and guilds, were busy turning the trees into toys and the toys into money. Merchants—passing along the main trade routes through such centers as Thuringia, Nuremberg, the Groeden valley, and Berchtesgaden—collected the wooden toys, and then sold them to the rest of the world. From the sixteenth century to the present day, German folk toys have been, and are still being, exported all over the world.

German folk toys have come to influence toymakers in other countries. Where the toys went, the German toymakers, shippers, traders, shopkeepers, and woodturners followed. It's no coincidence that countries as far apart as Taiwan, England, the United States, and Russia have long been making German-toy look-alikes!

Away with definitions—it is enough to know that woodturned folk toys hark back to a time when ordinary people made all manner of beautiful wooden toys on the lathe. The exciting thing is that, come terrible wars in the

Czechoslovakia, Krusnehory—A traditional "clatter" merry-go-round toy. The sides of the box are decorated with colored printed paper.

Czechoslovakia, Krusnehory—A "clatter" toy with turntable. Toys of this type were exported or smuggled across the border into Germany, to be sold in one of the big depots or trading centers.

Russian nesting dolls. Dolls of this type and character are still being made in Taiwan, Poland, Switzerland, and elsewhere.

nineteenth and twentieth centuries, horrendous political upheaval, the use of plastics, the invention of computer games, and all the rest, the humble woodturned folk toy continues to survive. Perhaps even more exciting—but not surprising—is that kids still enjoy playing with these toys!

This book is about personal, finger-tingling, involvement: the pleasures of handling tools, of smelling lengths of rough-sawn wood, of letting the tools cut the wood as it likes to be cut, of feeling the beautifully smooth round sections that come off the lathe. These are truly wonderful and very satisfying experiences that should not be missed.

By working through the various projects in this book, you will not only derive a great deal of personal pleasure in the doing, but better still, you will give pleasure to a great many kids—when you hand the toys over to your children, your grandchildren, your nephews, and nieces, your friends' children, and all the kids on your block. You can take if from us, there's nothing quite like the thrill of seeing the rough wood flow off as long ribbons, the square sections becoming smooth and round, and all the shapes—the wheels, bobbins, dowels, balls, knobs, and discs—become, as if by magic, beautiful toys.

If you have a lathe tucked away in a small cosy corner—in a shed, your basement or garage workshop—and if you have a yearning to make wooden toys, then this is the book for you. There's nothing to worry about, even if you are a raw beginner who doesn't know one end of the lathe from the other, our working drawings, how-to photographs, step-by-step hands-on illustrations, hints, tips and follow-ups, will show you the way.

Follow through our projects in order, and you will be able with some confidence to make everything from a jointed doll and a set of skittles to a rocking horse, a tractor, and many toys in between.

Just imagine it—a lathe, a chunk of wood, a few simple tools, and a selection of paints—and in a little time you will have made your own wonderful wooden toy.

What else to say, except be warned—the kids, the potential customers, and the curious will all soon be beating a path to your door! Best of luck.

Alan and Gillian Bridgewater

Tools, Techniques, and Materials

A–Z guides to woodturning and toymaking

WOODTURNING BASICS

Beads

Small decorative moulding elements that are convex or part circular in cross section. In the context of turned toymaking, beads are used to decorate dolls, wheels, spindles and such.

To cut a bead—
- Establish the limits of the bead by using the toe of the skew chisel to make V-cuts.
- Engage and run the heel of the skew down into the valley to cut away the sharp-angled shoulder.
- Make repeated cuts until you have a half-bead.
- Repeat the procedure for the other side of the bead.

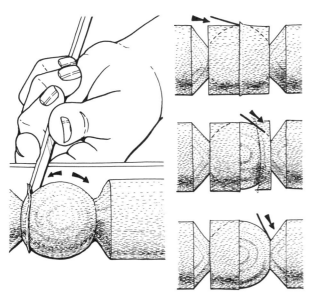

Beads.

Beeswax

A yellowish to dark brown wax secreted by honeybees—good nontoxic polish for small unpainted toys.

Between Centers

In the context of woodturning, the mounting of the workpiece between the forked headstock center and the pointed tailstock center—a technique used for turning dowels, spindles, balls, and long urn-like profiles.

Bevel

The angle that the shaft of a woodturning tool—a chisel or gouge—slopes back to the cutting edge. Long, small angled bevels are sharper, but then again, they lose their edge faster; gouges are best ground and honed to a bevel angle of about 45 degrees.

Blank

A prepared block, slab, or disc of wood—a piece of wood that is ready to be mounted on the lathe. Specialty suppliers sell bowl blanks, wheel blanks, spindle blanks, and so on; many suppliers will also cut a blank to your specifications.

Bowl

When you come to turn a bowl—with the wood mounted on a faceplate or screw chuck—it is best to use a square-cut gouge, meaning a gouge that is cut straight across at the end. That said, if you are a wary never-done-it-before beginner or are having trouble with the sharp corners of the gouge catching on the wood, then you could try using a round-nosed gouge and/or a round-nosed scraper. Certainly a round-nosed gouge isn't very efficient, but it will get the job done. The idea is that you gain confidence with the round-nosed gouge, and then—having understood why a square-cut gouge is the better tool for the task—you move on to the other tool.

Burning Centers

If you have a lathe with a straight forward-tapered tailstock center, and you find that the center friction burns the end of the workpiece, then ease the center back slightly, and oil the point of spin. If you intend doing a lot of turning, then you could get yourself a "live" center—meaning a revolving center with bearings.

Burnt Decoration

A form of decoration whereby the wood is scorched with a wire to create a brown color/texture—very good for making thin lines.

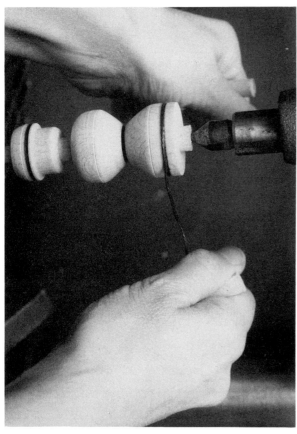

Burnt Decoration.

Centers

In a woodturning context, the pivotal points are described as "centers." The forked center is at the left-hand, or headstock, end of the lathe, whereas the pointed center is at the right-hand, or tailstock, end.

Centering and Roughing Out

Mounting the wood on the lathe and turning the initial cylinder/disc.

Chisel

Whereas gouges are used primarily for swiftly removing rough wood and for cutting into hollows, chisels—squared-ended and skew—are used for paring or skimming a surface to a nice, smooth finish. A skew chisel is one of the most important of all the woodturning tools. We favor using a wide long-pointed skew chisel for just about everything—except roughing out and the inside of bowls. In use, the blade is set flat down on the workpiece so that the back end or heel of the blade is looking in the direction of the cut—and then the handle is gently raised until the heel part of the bevel begins to catch and bite. At this point, the angle of the chisel is adjusted slightly until the waste comes off as a ribbon or streamer; then the tool is advanced. The greater the pressure and the slower the rate of advance, the greater the amount of wood that is cut away. By achieving a balance between pressure, the angle of the tool, and the rate of cut, it is possible to turn just about anything from a dowel, and a taper, to the back of a bowl, a decorative bead, a V-cut groove, and a ball. You need to master the skew chisel; so our best advice is that you have lots of try-outs until you know what's what.

Although we sometimes use the skew chisel flat down like a scraper—and there's no denying that it's a swift easy way of tidying up small curves—it does take the edge off the blade.

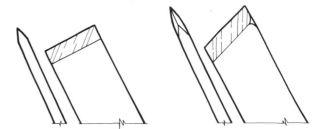

Chisel—(Left) Square-end chisel—edge and profile showing bevel angle (Right) Skew chisel—edge and profile showing bevel.

Chuck—Four-Jaw Chuck

In woodturning, a device used to hold the workpiece while it is being turned. The four jaws are screwed, in geared unison, towards the center to hold and position the workpiece. Although screw chucks are expensive, they are wonderfully efficient and time saving. We favor using a four-jaw chuck because it grips square-section wood without the need for prelathe preparation. Better still, with a little bit of ingenuity, such a chuck can be

10

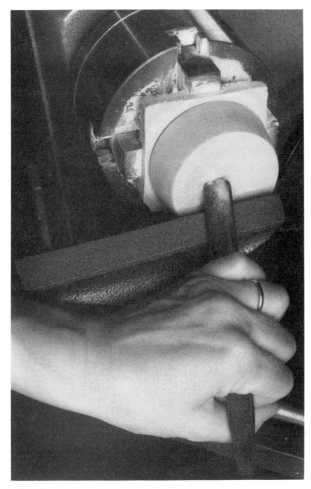

Chuck.

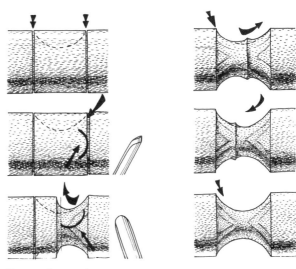

Cove—the cutting stages.

- Roll the gouge in a scooping motion so that the tool runs down into the valley.
- Rerun this procedure repeatedly on both sides of the valley or cove, until you have achieved the desired shape.

Discs

Toymakers need to make discs—for rolling wheels and steering wheels, base platforms, and so on ad infinitum. The swiftest way of making a large disc is to take a square-cut slab of wood, establish the center by drawing crossed diagonals, draw out the circle with a compass, cut away the bulk of the waste with a straight saw—or better still cut out the circle on a band saw—mount the wood on a faceplate or screw chuck, and then use a gouge to turn the disc down to a true finish.

used for just about every wood-holding task that you care to throw at it. Best of all, once the workpiece is in the chuck, you can rest assured that it's going to stay put. Note—don't be tempted to buy a three-jaw chuck—the three jaws won't grip square sections!

Close-Grained

Wood that has narrow annual rings—such wood tends to turn well.

Cove

To cut a cove—
- Mark out the size of the cove with dividers or the toe of the skew chisel.
- Lay the edge of the round-nosed gouge almost flat on the high point so that the inside of the gouge is looking towards the waste that needs to be cut away.

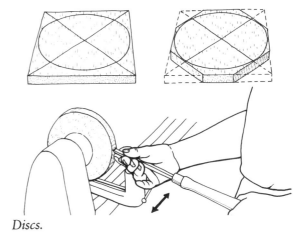

Discs.

Dividers

A two-legged compass-like instrument used for stepping off measurements. In woodturning, the heavy-duty dividers are set to an exact measurement—a step-off—and the two knife-sharp points are supported on the rest and held against the workpiece while it is in motion. The points mark the surface with small V-cut grooves.

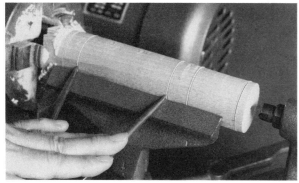

Dividers.

Drill Chuck

A gripping device—like the chuck on an electric drill—used at the tailstock end of the lathe, for holding and centering drill bits. In use, the workpiece is set in motion and the chuck-held drill is advanced so as to bore a centralized hole.

Faceplate

My lathe came with a six-inch faceplate to be used over the bed of the lathe, and a large faceplate to be used at the

Faceplate.

outboard end. In use, the bowl blanks are fixed to the plate with wood screws. The secret of success is to use short, fat screws, and to place them so that they do the minimum amount of damage to the back of the workpiece. Ideally, place the screws within an area that is going to be either covered up or cut away.

Gouges

In the context of woodturning, the gouge is a curve-sectioned blade used for most of the primary "roughing," or swift waste-removing tasks. The various gouge names tend to describe the function and/or the shape of the blade. There are . . . roughing gouges, bowl gouges, spindle gouges, round-nosed gouges, and so on.

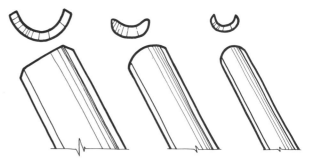

Gouges—Blade cross sections and profiles.

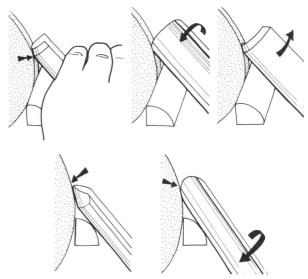

Grinding—A square-cut gouge (top, left to right); Hold the gouge so that the bevel is at the correct 45 degree angle—swivel the blade so that the whole bevel is at the same angle, first one way, and then the other. A round-nosed gouge (bottom, left to right); Hold the blade at the correct 25 to 30 degree angle—roll and swivel the blade to cut the angle and profile.

Grinding

The act of using a grindstone to bring the bevel to the correct angle and finish. Be very careful not to burn the edge of the bevel. Being mindful that the best way of learning is by doing, best to spend time trying out different angles and finishes.

Headstock

The headstock is the power-driven unit at the left-hand end of the lathe. The headstock carries two thrust bearings in which the spindle or mandrel revolves. The power is supplied to the spindle by means of an electric motor and a drive belt. The spindle has an external screw for chucks and faceplates, and an internal taper for the pronged center.

Lathe

A woodworking machine for cutting and shaping round sections. The wood is pivoted between centers or held in a chuck, while a hand-held tool advances and makes a cut.

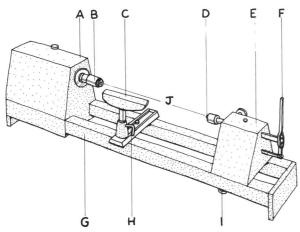

Lathe—Parts of the lathe; (A) Headstock. (B) Spindle and drive center. (C) Tool rest. (D) Tailstock center. (E) Tailstock. (F) Spindle advance. (G) Lathe bed. (H) Quick-action clamp for the tool rest. (I) Adjustment nut for the tailstock. (J) Distance between centers.

Lathe Safety

The lathe is potentially an extremely dangerous piece of equipment. Before you switch on, always—
- Make sure that the workpiece is well mounted and secure.
- Turn the workpiece over by hand, and make sure that it is clear of the tool rest.

Lathe Safety—When you are polishing with wax and a cloth—make a pad—never roll the cloth around your fingers.

- Tie back your hair, roll up your sleeves, and generally make sure that you aren't going to get dragged into the equipment.
- Make sure that children and pets are out of harm's way.

When you have switched on the power, always—
- Stop or, at least, slow down before testing with a template, divider, or calliper.
- Move the tool rest well out of the way before sanding.
- Wear a mask and safety goggle or, better still, a respirator.
- Make sure that your chosen wood is nontoxic—for you, the turner, and for the child when he/she gets to play with the toy.
- Hold all the tools firmly.
- Make sure that the cut-off switch is working and within reach.
- Never reach out over the lathe while it is running.
- When you are polishing with wax and a cloth, never roll the cloth around your fingers, but rather make a pad.

There are, of course, many more hazards—everything from poisonous wood dust to tools falling off shelves and the workpiece flying off the lathe. All you can do is always be wide awake and ready for the unexpected.

Note—don't worry too much about wood flying off the lathe—in my experience, it tends to fall down rather than forward.

13

Parting Off.

Parting Off

The act of using a parting tool to part a finished component off from the lathe.

Roughing Out

The act of using the gouge to swiftly turn the square section of wood down to a cylindrical/round section. As my lathe is pretty hefty, I usually—

• Find the end centers of the square section of wood by drawing crossed diagonals.

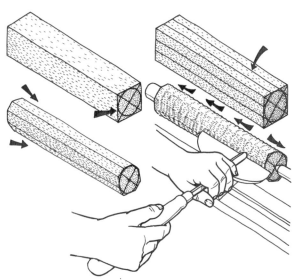

Roughing out—Find the center by drawing crossed diagonals, and draw a circle. (Top right) Draw tangents at the circle-diagonal intersections to create an octagon, and draw lines along the length of the wood to mark out the waste. (Bottom left) Cut away the waste. (Bottom right) Use a gouge to swiftly turn the wood down to a rough round section.

14

• Mount the wood on the lathe.
• Turn the wood down to a rough cylinder with a gouge.
   If you only have a small lathe, best if, having found the end center points of the wood, you—
• Scribe out circles with a compass.
• Draw tangents at the circle-diagonal cross-over points.
• Draw lines along the length of the wood to establish the waste areas.
• Plane off the waste—
all before mounting the wood on the lathe.

Rubbing Down

To rub the wood down while it is mounted on the lathe. To use a series of graded sandpapers/emery papers to achieve a smooth ready-to-paint finish.

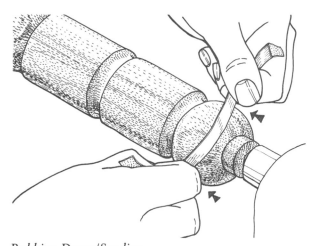

Rubbing Down/Sanding.

Sanding

The act of using a sandpaper/emery paper to rub the wood down to a smooth finish. As a good deal of the sanding is done while the wood is still on the lathe—meaning it's done in an enclosed space—I usually wear a respirator. When the sanding is complete, I usually brush myself down, wipe the workpiece over with a slightly damp cloth, and move to a special dust-free area that we have set aside for painting.

Scrapers

For turning very hard woods, and/or for small details like rings and beads, you might well decide to use a scraper rather than a gouge or chisel. In scraping, the whole blade touches the wood—straight-on or slightly downwards. If you are a cautious beginner, you might be better off using scrapers inasmuch as the scraping technique is not difficult to master. Scrapers come in many shapes and sizes, many of them designed for specific tasks. For example, the round-nosed scraper is good for cutting small hollows, the hooked beak-like scraper is used for cutting rings and beads, and so on. Traditionally, many toymakers design, grind, and modify scraper blanks so that they always cut the same profile.

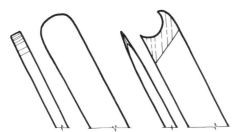

Scrapers—(Left) Round-nosed scraper—edge and profile. (Right) Hooked-beak scraper, used for cutting rings and beads—edge and profile.

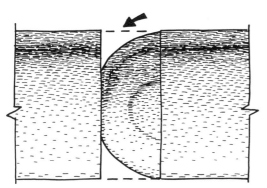

Shoulder—round shoulder—term used to describe a specific spindle-turned profile.

Sharpening

It's most important that turning chisels and gouges be kept razor sharp. To this end, I have mounted a sheet of fine-grade emery cloth on a nine-inch disc of ½-inch thick plywood, at the center of which there is a disc of leather, flesh side out, about six inches in diameter, and an even smaller disc of leather with smooth side out, about four-inches in diameter. All looking a bit like a target. The whole works is screwed and mounted on a faceplate on the outboard end of the lathe. In use, I first stroke the blade on the emery cloth, and then strop the bevel edge to a finish on the two inner leather discs. The whole operation is over in a few seconds, without having to move away from the lathe.

Shoulder

To cut a round shoulder—
• Indent a line with the toe of the skew chisel.
• Lay the chisel flat down on the high point.
• Engage the heel and run the chisel in a smooth rolling action down into the valley.

Sizing

The act of using callipers, dividers, a template, or whatever, to fix the size—the diameter or profile—of a turning. I usually make step-offs with a pair of dividers, measure cylinder diameters with a pair of callipers, and transfer shapes, steps, and profiles with a template.

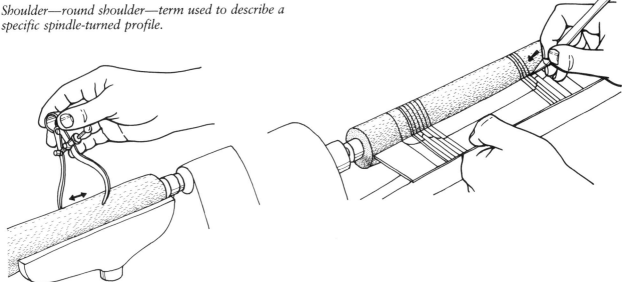

Sizing—Use a pair of callipers (left) to size or measure the diameter of a cylinder. Use a cardboard template (right) to transfer shapes and measurements to the wood.

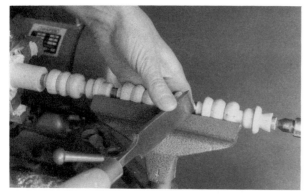

Skew chisel—Use the point, or "toe," to cut-in fine angles and V-cuts.

Skew Chisel

In the context of woodturning, a skew chisel has bevels on both faces and angled edges. Once the wood has been turned to a round section with a gouge, then the skew chisel is used variously to shape and smooth the turning. The point of the blade is termed the "toe" and the back the "heel."

Spigot

A short, cylindrical projection or step on one component, designed to fit into a hole on another—a very important feature in many turned wooden toys. Sometimes simply called a round tenon.

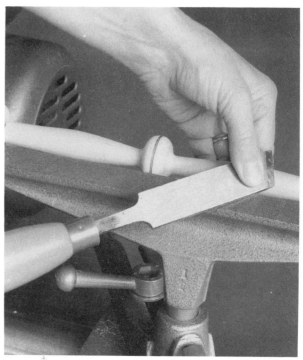

Skew chisel—Use the back part of the blade, or the "heel," to skim off thin shavings.

Tapered Work

To cut a taper—
• First turn the wood down to a cylinder.
• Make a number of sizing cuts to fix the primary diameters—at top and bottom, and maybe halfway along.
• Set the skew chisel flat down at the top of the hill, and face the heel part of the bevel so that it looks in the direction of the cut.
• Take progressive bites downhill.

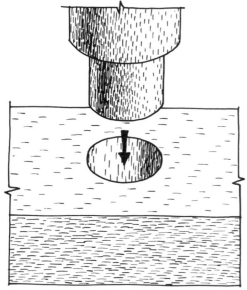

Spigot—The shoulder butts against body of the wood and makes for a strong, stable toymaking joint.

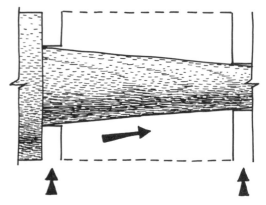

Taper.

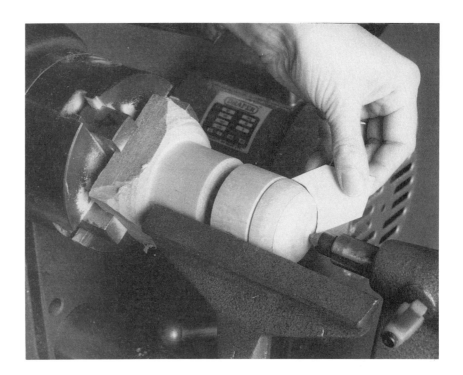

Template—Use the part-circle template to check the half-ball shape.

Template

A cardboard shape or profile, used to check a turned shape.

Tool Rest

The T-shaped rest on which you pivot and support your hand and/or the shaft of the tool. All that is required for maximum efficiency is that the rest be as close as possible to the workpiece, and set so that the bevel of your tool is on the work. You could, if you prefer, switch off the lathe, set the bevel against the wood, adjust the height of the rest so that the tool is supported, and then switch on the power and take it from there.

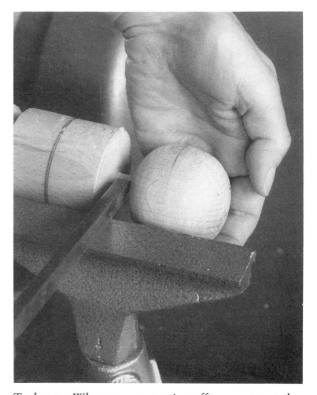

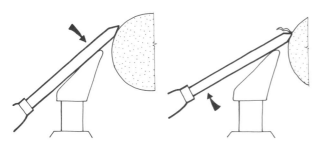

Tool rest—(Left) Support the tool on the rest and lower the handle until the bevel is resting on the spinning wood. (Right) Bring the handle up until the blade begins to bite, and then advance the cut.

Tool rest—When you are parting off, you support the tool on the rest, while at the same time cupping and easing the workpiece away from you with the other hand—in this instance the tool rest acts as a third hand.

17

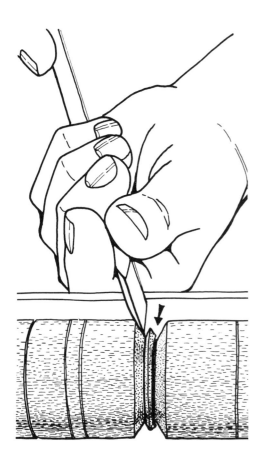

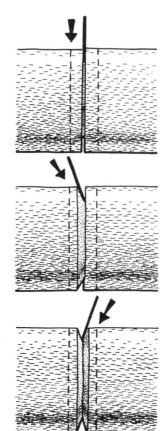

V-cuts—(Top right) Use the toe of the skew chisel to fix the middle of the cut. (Middle right) Run the chisel at an angle into the initial cut to make one half of the V. (Right bottom) Run the chisel in at the other side to complete the cut. (Left) If you want to make a wider and deeper V-cut, then run through the first steps again.

V-Cuts

To make a V-cut—
- First run the toe of the skew chisel into the wood at the point where you want the narrowest diameter to be—at the deepest part of the valley.
- Lay the bevel to the side of the initial cut.
- Engage the heel.
- Roll the tool down into the wood to cut away the waste, and so that the heel finishes up at the bottom of the valley.
- Make several bites; do this on both sides, until you get it right.

Workshop

In the context of woodturning, your workshop might be anything from a shed to a lean-to shelter out in the garden, or part of the basement or garage—as long as it has light and power. The noise, dust, and debris associated with a lathe need to be carefully considered. We keep our lathe in a garden shed workshop; we do the cutting, sawing, drilling, and sanding in one end of the same shed, but we do the final painting in the house.

A–Z guide to toymaking

TOYMAKING BASICS

Acrylic Paint

A plastic polyvinyl-acetate-type paint that is easy to use, water-based, and quick-drying. Acrylics are perfect for toymaking, because they can be used straight from the can, the colors are bright, they dry swiftly, and, most important of all with respect to children, they are non-toxic. As toys get a lot of handling, it's a good idea to protect the painted surfaces with a couple of well-brushed coats of clear high-gloss varnish.

Band Saw

A power-operated tool consisting of an endless-metal-loop blade running over and driven by a number of wheels—a good tool for cutting disc blanks in preparation for turning. If you aim to do a lot of woodturning/toymaking, a band saw ought to be fairly high on your tools-to-get list.

Bench

Although a woodturning toymaker does need a good bench, all that is actually required is a stable wooden surface that is strong enough to take a vise along with a variety of clamps and holdfasts.

Brushes

Paintbrushes come in many shapes and sizes. We prefer to use the soft long-haired brushes used by watercolor artists. If you use acrylic paints, then always wash the brushes immediately after use, and store them bristle up.

Callipers

A two-legged compass-like instrument used primarily for gauging diameters—usually consists of two C-shaped legs that are pivoted at the crotch, or two S shapes that are crossed and pivoted to make a figure eight.

Clamps

Screw devices for securing wood while it is being worked are called variously clamps, cramps, C-clamps, hold-fasts, hold-downs, and any number of trade names.

Clasp Knife

Just about any folding knife used in turning/toymaking—we favour the use of small penknives.

Compass or a Pair of Compasses

Two-legged instruments used for drawing circles and arcs—best to get a long-legged screw-operated type.

Coping Saw

A small frame handsaw used for cutting thin small-section wood. The G-shaped frame allows the thin blade to be swiftly fitted and removed. A good saw for cutting curved profiles, and enclosed "windows." If you aim to do a lot of woodturning and toymaking, then get yourself a coping saw as well as a scroll saw and a band saw.

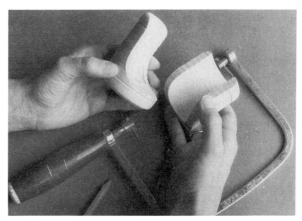

Coping saw.

Designing

Working out a structure, pattern, or form by making drawings, sketches, outlines and/or prototypes. When we see an unusual or exciting traditional toy in a museum, or maybe in an old book or painting, we make sketches; then we build the toy up swiftly from rough wood, before we finalize the design or use special wood. In many instances—especially if we can't actually get to handle the toy—the only way to find out how it operates is to make a working model.

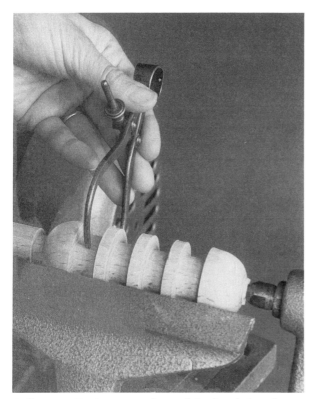

Callipers—Beginners are best advised to bring the wood to a halt before checking the diameters with callipers.

Drilling holes—If you want to bore out a smooth-sided hole—one with a blind or flat bottom—then you can't do better than use a Forstner bit.

Drilling Holes

In the context of toymaking, holes need to be clean edged, smooth sided, and sometimes blind or flat bottomed. This being the case, we favor using Forstner bits in a drill press or bench drill.

Dust-Free

Before you start painting, make sure that the workpiece is free from wood dust and debris. Sweep up the debris, vacuum the surfaces, wipe the workpiece with a damp cloth, and then move to a dust-free area in preparation for painting. We like to keep the woodworking and the painting completely separate. Our woodturning workshop is at one end of the garden, and our painting room is in the house.

Elevations

In drawing, the views of an object. A particular elevation or view might be described as "top," "end," or "side."

End Grain

Cross-section grain at the end of a piece of timber—the section seen when you make a clean cut through a tree. End grain is difficult to turn and to work; it needs to be approached with care.

Finishing

The act of scraping, rubbing down with sandpaper, painting, waxing, and otherwise enhancing the appearance of the project. Being mindful that young children like to explore toys with their mouths, tongues, and noses, it's vital that the toys be completely smooth to the touch—no splinters, sharp edges, or points. That said, some of the toys in this book—as with many shop bought toys—are intended only for *carefully supervised play*.

Forstner Bit

Drill bits used for drilling out smooth-sided, flat-bottomed holes—sizes range from $\frac{3}{8}$ inch to $3\frac{1}{2}$ inches in diameter. We use Forstner bits for almost all our drilling tasks.

Forstner drill bits come in a wide range of sizes.

Glues and Adhesives

Although there are all manner of glues and adhesives—everything from animal glues to instant glues and resins—we favor using Super Glue for small areas and for "tacking," and PVA, meaning polyvinyl acetate, for general work.

Grain

Meaning the annual rings that run though the wood—all the lines, colors, and textures that go to characterize a piece of wood. Woodturners and toymakers spend a good deal of their time trying to work out how to approach the grain to best advantage—will it cut? Will it splinter? Is it strong enough for the task at hand? and so on. That said, since most of the toys in this book are painted, you can, for the most part, forget about good-to-look-at woods, and, instead, concentrate your attention on woods that are easy to turn.

Green Wood

Wood that still contains sap—unseasoned wood. Green wood is wonderfully easy to turn; the only problem is that, once it has been turned, it continues to dry out to the extent that the turned pieces generally warp, split, and fall to bits.

Gridded Working Drawing

A scaled, square grid placed over a working drawing. In use the object illustrated can be reduced or enlarged simply by changing the scale of the grid. For example, if the grid is described as "one square to one inch," and you want to double the scale, then all you do is read off each square as being equal to two inches. When you come to transferring the drawing to the wood, you just draw out a grid at the suggested size and transfer the contents of each square. At four grid squares to one inch, you draw out a ¼-inch grid—where one square is ¼ inch. (You might also consider making use of an office-type photo-copying machine that can reduce or enlarge the original—and then simply transfer the new-sized drawing directly to the wood or use it to step off measurements to the turning workpiece with dividers.)

Hardwood

Botanically speaking, hardwood comes from broad-leafed deciduous trees. In many ways, since hardwoods aren't necessarily harder in substance or even harder to work than softwoods, the term is only meaningful in describing very general characteristics.

Inspirational Designs and Material

Meaning our sources—all the traditional woodturned toys that we see in museums, collections, old books, and magazines. It's a good idea to keep a sketchbook/scrapbook and to make notes and sketches whenever you see something interesting. We draw most of our inspiration from museum originals. However, we should make it clear that we do not actually copy designs; the process of creating our own design involves studying forms, movements, profiles, and such as we gradually come up with new ideas or at least interesting variations on old themes.

Be Warned—If you intend to sell the toys you make, be careful not to use proprietary (copyrighted or patented) material. Generally, it is safe to say that you *can copy and sell* traditional toys found in museum collections. But, be sure to do proper research for other sources; you *can't just copy and sell* toys found in the local art gallery, contemporary catalogues, or some other publication without explicit permission.

Marking Out

Using a sharp-point pencil/dividers to make guidelines.

Masking Tape

A general-purpose adhesive tape used variously to mark out midlines, measure around curved surfaces, hold components while they are being sawn, glued, painted, etc.

Measure

Might be anything from a wooden ruler, metal rule, to a flexible tape, or even a piece of string.

Modifying

Changing and redesigning a project so that it is changed—bigger, smaller, worked from thicker or thinner wood, made to use shop bought wheels, or whatever. Many traditional toy designs need to be modified, especially in the interests of child safety.

Off-Cuts

Small pieces of usable wood left over after you have made the project. If you intend making a lot of toys, then you might well search out a supply of someone elses off-cuts—say from a joiner or furniture maker.

Paints and Painting

Before painting, always clear away bench clutter, wipe up dust, and carefully set out all your tools and materials so that they are comfortably at hand. We prefer to use acrylic colors protected with a couple of coats of clear varnish. (See Acrylics)

Be Warned—In the context of toymaking, you must never use odds and ends of old oil paint—as might be found, say, in grandpa's workshop. Certainly such paints are often in good condition and beautifully luscious, but that's because they contain metallic oxides *such as lead*. For very young put-everything-in-their-mouths children, such materials are *highly poisonous*! If you do want to use household paints, then make sure that the paint is suitable for toys. If you intend making toys for sale, you must contact health and safety officials for any questionable substance and ask their advice.

Pencil-Press Transferring

The act of tracing a master design, and then pencil-pressing the traced lines to the wood.

Putting Together

Meaning to actually assemble the various component parts, and/or to assess the work in progress, perhaps, to critically rethink the design.

Sanding Disc

I have fitted a sanding disc to the outboard end of the lathe—it's a very swift way to shape wood. Only thing is, it's so dusty that I need to wear a respirator.

Be Warned—Large amounts of fine wood dust are hazardous—bad for your eyes, skin, and lungs.

Scroll Saw

A power-driven, fine-bladed bench saw—sometimes called a jigsaw or fretsaw—used for cutting small-section wood. In use, the workpiece is pushed across the worktable and fed into the blade. The blades come in many grades and are easy and cheap to replace. The super-fast, up-and-down jiggling action of the blade results in a swift, fine, safe cut. If you enjoy making small wooden toys, then, second to a lathe, you need a scroll saw.

Setting In

The process or procedure of transferring the working drawings to the face of the wood and making the initial cuts.

Tracing Paper

A strong translucent paper used for tracing. We usually work up a good design, take a tracing with a soft 2B pencil, line-in the reverse side of the tracing, and then rework the lines with a hard pencil to transfer the lines to the wood.

Work-Out Paper

Inexpensive paper as might be used for initial roughs and work-outs—best to use slightly matte white paper.

Vise

A bench-mounted clamp.

PROJECTS

•1•

Baby Doll

A simple, spindle-turned skittle doll, with painted imagery

Kids love dolls! A doll to kiss, a doll to cuddle, a doll to talk to—most of us have, at some time or other, enjoyed the bedtime, playtime comfort of a toy doll.

1–1   Project picture.

The wonderful thing is that a doll doesn't need to be a hugely expensive item with hinged limbs, golden curls, and so on—small children, especially, are well able to breathe life into the most basic figures.

Although this doll draws her inspiration from such archetypes as American Puritan poupard dolls, the small dolls as made by the Native American Hopi people, and even ancient Egyptian clay dolls, we think that, primarily, she has her roots in all the beautiful lathe-turned skittle and pestle dolls that were made in England and Europe from earliest times to the beginning of the twentieth century (see 1–1). That is to say, she has a simple turned and painted form—just a body and a head—she looks to be dressed in "swaddling-clothes."

Dolls of this type and character must surely be the best buy around! Children like them, because the design allows for unlimited imaginative play—they can be soldiers, or babies, or skittles, or whatever takes the child's fancy. Parents like them because they are safe, almost indestructible, and inexpensive, and woodturners like them, because they can be turned from scrap, made in a few moments, and, perhaps, sold at a good profit.

So there you go, if you know of a child who wants a doll, if you have a workshop full of small off-cuts, and, if you like making simple, strong, bold, spindle-turned forms, then this project is going to keep you busy!

THOUGHTS ON DESIGN AND TECHNIQUE

Once you have considered all the tool and material implications of the project, have a look at the working drawings (see 1–2), and see how, at a scale of four grid squares to one inch, the doll stands about 6½ inches high and a little over 1½ inches in diameter. Note the simple spindle form, the ball-turned head, and the smooth tapered or cove cuts that go to make the decorative features at the neck and the base. Consider how the strength of the form relies on the turning being cleanly and confidently worked.

Lathe and Tool Considerations

Although I use a four-jaw chuck, this is one of those projects that can quite easily be turned between centers. If you are a beginner working on a small lathe, and if you are looking for a good straightforward, inexpensive starter project, then this could well be the project for you.

Tools and Equipment

Apart from a lathe, you need—
- small round-nosed gouge
- parting tool
- skew chisel
- both dividers and callipers
- pencil and ruler
- sheet each of tracing and workout paper
- pack of graded sandpapers
- two soft-haired watercolor paintbrushes—broad and fine point
- acrylic paints in the colors dark blue, black, yellow, green, beige pink, red, gold, and white
- small quantity of clear high-gloss varnish

Wood

For this project you need a nine-inch length of hard, dense-grained wood two by two inches square. Although we have gone for beech, you could just as well choose an easier-to-turn wood such as jelutong or lime/linden/basswood.

As always, when you are making toys—especially small "cuddle" items that are intended for toddlers—you do have to be mindful that the toy is likely to be sucked and chewed. You have to make absolutely sure, of course, that the wood is splinter resistant, colorfast, and non-toxic. If you have any doubts at all about your choice of wood, then ask the advice of a specialist wood supplier.

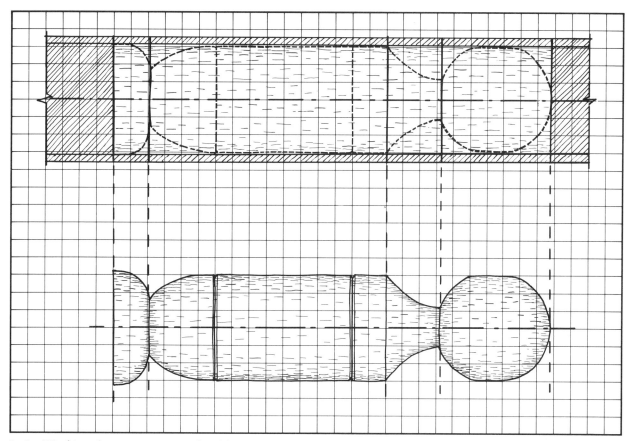

1–2 *Working drawings—at a scale of four grid squares to one inch, the finished doll stands about 6½ inches high and 1½ inches wide at the base. Note how the simple stylized forms all relate to the most common primary cuts.*

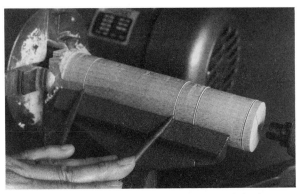

1–3 Allow 3½ inches between the top of the base and the bottom of the neck.

1–4 Set in a 1⅝-inch step-off for the head.

TOYMAKING STAGES

Mounting the Wood on the Lathe and First Cuts

After you have had a good look at skittle turned dolls, in general, and this doll, in particular, and once you have gathered together all your tools and materials, draw the design at full size, making a clear tracing (see 1–2). And, of course, if you have in mind making the doll bigger or giving her a few extra curves or whatever, then this is the time to include such modifications in the design.

Take your chosen length of wood, make sure that it is completely free from knots, splits, stains, and such, establish the end centers by drawing crossed diagonals on the ends, and mount it securely on the lathe. This done, bring the tool rest up as near as possible to the work, set out your tools so that they are comfortably at hand, and generally make sure that everything is in good, safe working order. To this end, roll up your sleeves, tie back your hair, see to it that the ON/OFF switch works, make sure that the floor is clear of trip-up bits and pieces, and so on.

Woodturning Tip

Where to keep your turning tools? It's a bit of a problem. If they are higher than the lathe, then they might fall down onto the spinning wood. If they are under the bed of the lathe, then they get buried in shavings. I have settled for having them behind me.

Once you are sure that all is correct, switch on the power. Take the round gouge, and swiftly turn down the corners of waste to achieve a rough cylinder. This done, take the skew chisel, and turn the rough cylinder down to a smooth finish. Aim for a diameter of about 1½ inches.

Setting-In the Step-Offs and Turning the Coves, Curves, and Hollows

With the wood turned down to a smooth finish, take the dividers, and carefully set out all the step-offs that go to make up the design (see 1–3). Working from left to right along the workpiece, that is, from the foot of the figure to the head, allow a small amount for headstock/chuck waste, and then set out the primary step-offs in the order ½ inch for the foot, 3½ inches for the distance between the top of the base and the bottom of the neck, ¾ inch for the neck, 1⅝ inches for the head, and the remainder for tailstock waste (see 1–4).

Woodturning Tip

The divider is best sharpened so that the arms come to a knife point. The idea is, that the flat point makes a thin cut, rather than a ragged scratch.

Once you have set-in the primary step-off points with shallow V-cuts, then comes the very pleasurable task of turning the forms. Starting with the head, fix the divider to ⅞ inch, and mark out a step-off that halves the 1¾ inch head (see 1–5, top). This done, take the skew chisel, and, working with the heel, start to turn the two beads—or half-balls—that go to make the ball shape. Note that the head isn't a true ball or sphere. Use the toe of the skew to indent and deepen the lines that mark out the top of the head and the neck. Take the parting tool and make sizing cuts to define the top and bottom of the head (see 1–5, bottom). Try to envision the head and neck areas. Be careful not to remove too much waste wood at this stage, and avoid having a "stepped" look to the neck. Use the heel of the skew chisel to cut the curves down into the valleys (see 1–6).

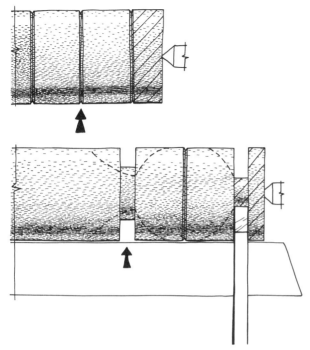

1–5 (Top) Mark out a step-off that halves the 1⅝-inch head. (Bottom) Take the parting tool and define the width of the neck with a sizing cut.

Woodturning Tip

When you come to the final smoothing, cup the work-piece with your fingers, while at the same time pressing the tool down with your thumb. Try to "feel" the cutting action and the quality of the resultant finish.

The procedure is to set the bevel part of the heel on the high point of the ball, lift and twist the chisel handle until the cutting edge begins to bite, and twist and roll the heel down-and-round the curve and into the valley—until the blade is in the vertical position.

When you have made a series of successive cuts to turn one half of the ball, then turn the chisel over, lay the other side of the bevel on the high point, and repeat the procedure to cut the other half.

To turn the beautiful smooth-curved cove shape that goes to make the neck, lay the round-nosed gouge almost flat on its side, on the high point of the neck—meaning the line of the shoulder—and engage the blade to start the cut. Cut a little groove for the blade to rest in, and roll the blade in a scooping motion so that the bottom of the bevel leans on the wood (see 1–7). As you gradually cut deeper into the valley, roll the gouge, until the bevel finishes up on its back at the bottom of the bevel.

1–6 The heel of skew chisel is used to cut the curves down into the valleys.

1–7 Roll the blade in an easy scooping motion, so that the bevel leans in on the wood.

Once you have turned the curved cove shape of the neck, take the skew chisel, turn it over so that the heel is uppermost, and use the toe to clean out the sharp angle between the narrowest part of the neck, and the underside of the head (see 1–8). Having cut the neck, then use the heel of the skew to clean up and define the point where the cylinder meets the shoulder. Aim for a nice crisp angle (see 1–9).

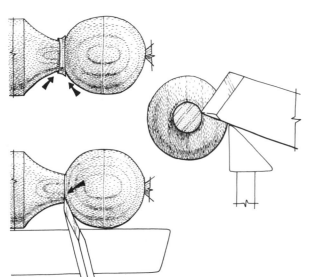

1–8   Cleaning the sharp angle between the head and the neck—(Top) Run the toe of the skew chisel in from both directions. (Right, side view) Make sure that the point of contact is slightly above the axis of spin. (Bottom, top view) Angle the toe of the tool around the curve—as needed, use the point of the tool like a scraper.

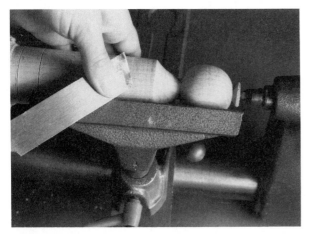

1–9   Use your fingers to steady the workpiece and your thumb to steady the tool—try to "feel" the cutting action.

Take the skew chisel, set-in the V-cut about 1½ inches up from the bottom of the base, and deepen the V-cut at the foot (see 1–10, top). Turn down the two shoulders—or you might say reversed half-balls—that go to make the shape of the base/foot (see 1–10, bottom). Hone the skew chisel razor sharp, and bring the whole workpiece to a cleanly skimmed finish. Finally, nip in the little V-cut groove that sets out the line of the "shoulder."

FINISHING AND PAINTING

Once you have turned what you consider is a well-featured, nicely finished doll, use the fine-grade sandpaper to rub the whole workpiece down to a super-smooth finish. Spend time getting it right. Take the parting tool, and very carefully part the doll from the lathe.

Woodturning Tip

If you are turning between centers—meaning without a wood-holding chuck—first use the skew or parting tool to part the head of the doll from the tailstock waste, and then saw the base free from the waste after the workpiece is off the lathe.

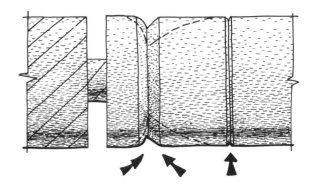

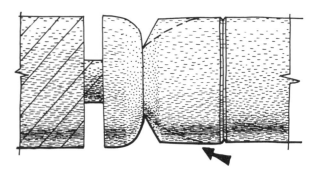

1–10   (Top) Set-in the V-cut at about 1½ inches up from the bottom of the base, and deepen the V-cut at the foot. (Bottom) To complete the second curve, cut in the direction of the arrow.

Sand the parting-off points to a good finish, make sure that the doll stands upright, wipe away all the dust, and move to the dust-free area that you have set aside for painting. Have a look at the painting grid (see 1–11). Start by laying on the main areas of ground color—black for the base/foot, blue for the body, and beige pink for the shoulders and head. As needed—and not forgetting to give the paint a light sanding between coats—lay on a second coat for a good dense cover. Next, paint the yellow hair, the red flower centers, the white petals on the body, and all the other little decorative details that go to make the design. Pay particular attention to the face details—the red lips, the happy-mouth shape, big open eyes, and blush on the cheeks.

Finally, when you have variously painted in the details, signed and dated the base—and maybe painted in a name and anything else that takes your fancy—then, lay on a couple of coats of varnish. The doll is finished and ready for the nursery!

TROUBLESHOOTING AND POSSIBLE MODIFICATIONS

If you decide to use paints other than acrylics, then make sure that they are completely safe and nontoxic. In the context of toys, never be tempted to use leftover domestic paint. I say this, because some household/boat/auto paints do contain toxic materials.

- Prior to painting, press three thumbtacks into the base of each skittle—like little feet—so that, while the paint/varnish is wet, the skittle doesn't come into contact with the work surface.
- If you decide to change the design, be mindful that small children are always going to try to put the doll where it doesn't belong—in their eyes, up their nose, and so on. This being so, it is best to avoid thin, long

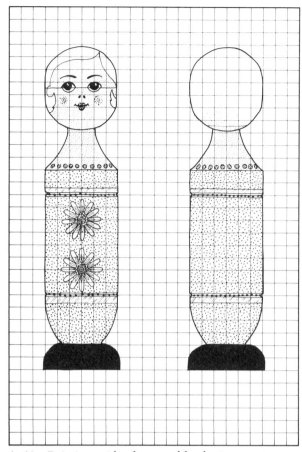

1–11 *Painting grid—front and back views—at a scale of four grid squares to one inch.*

forms, sharp points, and sharp edges. That said, kids are always going to try the unexpected!

- To help the skittle stand square and upright, it's a good idea to slightly undercut and "dish" the base.

• 2 •

Lady Doll Shaker

A hollow-turned shaker rattle with dried-pea noisemakers and lady doll imagery

Rattles and shakers are good, fun items! Woodturners get a huge kick out of making them, and kids like playing with them. This shaker doll is a real beauty, and rather special on quite a few counts (see 2–1). From the child's

2–1 Project picture.

viewpoint, it is more than a shaker and doll to cuddle; it is, best of all, a doll that "whispers." What makes the soft sound? How did the noisemakers get inside the lady? Does it open? Once a child gets his or her hands on this project, a lot of questions will be asked!

Much the same goes for the woodturner. It is one of those projects that begs questions. Where is the lid? How do you get the peas inside the shaker? Is it made all-of-a-piece?—and so on.

THOUGHTS ON DESIGN AND TECHNIQUE

After you have considered the tool and material requirements of making a project of this size and character, have a good long look at the working drawings (see 2–2) and other illustrations, and make decisions about size and technique. Ask yourself whether your lathe is big enough. Can you manage without a chuck? Would you prefer to make the image larger or smaller? Consider all the possibilities, and then, in the light of your tool kit and your experience, decide what you want the project to be. If necessary, modify the drawings to suit your needs.

Having sorted out in your own mind just how you want the project to go, have another look at the working drawings (see 2–2). Note, how—in the making—the lady is held in a four-jaw chuck, the base-plug is parted off, the workpiece is removed from the lathe and bored out with a Forstner bit, and the base-plug is refitted.

Be mindful that the success of the project hinges on the feature that, once the base-plug has been made and the body of the lady bored out, the whole works can be recentered on the lathe. This is not to say that this procedure is especially difficult—just a little bit tricky—but it does need to be done with care.

Be Warned—If the wood is badly off-center, then the act of returning the body of the lady might well result in the walls of the dress—the hollow part—becoming too thin.

Lathe and Tool Considerations

Again, I favor using a four-jaw chuck, because the turning procedures are that much easier if the headstock end of the workpiece is supported. For example, with this project, when you come to turn the base-plug, it's so much easier if the bulk of the wood is going to stay put once the base is parted off. That said, if you need to work with the wood held between centers, then no problem—you simply take the turning to within a hair's breadth of completion, and then remove the wood from the lathe, before parting off with a saw.

In many ways, the working stages of this project—the procedures and techniques—are ordered by whether or not you have the use of a large diameter Forstner drill bit. If you can't get to use such a bit, then you have to work out another way of boring out the body. It's not too much of a problem if the workpiece is held securely in a chuck, but otherwise the project needs thinking about!

Tools and Equipment

Apart from a lathe, you need—
- round-nosed gouge
- parting tool
- skew chisel
- large Forstner bit—ours is 2⅛ inches in diameter
- bench drill press
- both dividers and callipers
- pencil and ruler
- sheet each of tracing and workout paper
- pack of graded sandpapers
- two soft-haired watercolor paintbrushes—broad and fine point
- acrylic paints in the colors dark blue, light blue, white, pink, red, and black
- small quantity of clear high-gloss varnish
- handful of dried peas/rice
- Super Glue

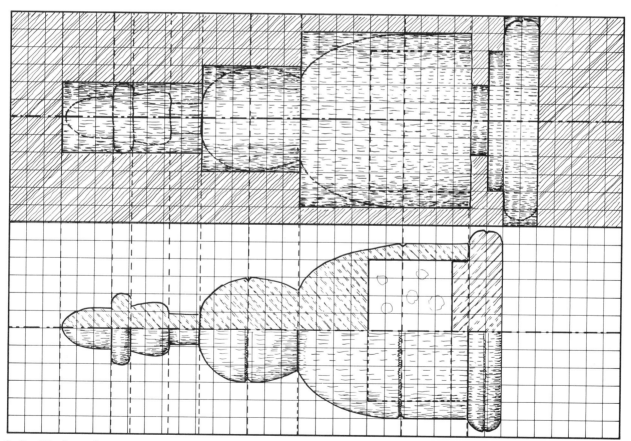

2–2 *Working drawings—at a scale of four grid squares to one inch, the finished doll stands about 6½ inches high and almost three inches across the widest diameter at the base. Note the width of the base-plug step/spigot, and how it needs to be parted off at an early stage.*

Wood

For this project you need a 10-inch length of hard, dense-grained wood at three by three inches square. Ideally it needs to be a soft, light-in-weight, easy-to-turn wood like jelutong or lime/linden/basswood. Again, you do have to be aware that as the wood is likely to be sucked and chewed—more so with a toy for a very small child—so it must be splinter resistant, colorfast, and nontoxic. Finally, and this is especially important in a tricky project that's going to be hollow-turned, it's important that the wood be free from splits, cavities, and knots. If you have any doubts, ask your supplier.

TOYMAKING STAGES

Setting Out the Wood and First Cuts

When you have gathered all your tools and materials, and drawn and traced the design to size, fix the end center points by drawing crossed diagonals, and mount the wood on the lathe. Bring the tool rest up to the work, and turn the wood over by hand—just to make sure that the rest is well positioned. By this I mean make sure that the rest is slightly lower than the center of spin and just clear of the wood.

Having checked that all is correct, and set out your tools so that they are comfortably at hand, pin up your drawings so that they are in view, switch on the power, and to work.

Woodturning Tip

If you are a beginner to woodturning, then it's a good idea to write down and follow a pre-switch-on checklist.

Start by taking the gouge—either a square or a round nosed—and turning the whole length of the wood down to a smooth cylinder. Aim for a cylinder that is, as near as possible, three inches in diameter.

When you have turned a crisp, clean-cut cylinder, take the divider and transfer the measurements from the working drawing/tracing to the wood. Working from left to right and with the head end of the doll being nearest to the chuck, take the divider and transfer the step-offs in sequence; about two inches for headstock waste, ¾ inch for the hat, ⅜ inch for the hat brim, ⅝ inch for the face/head, ⅜ inch for the neck, 1⅜ inch for the top of the body, 2½ inches for the skirt, ¼ inch for waste, ¼ inch for the spigot part of the plug, ½ inch for the base, and the rest for tailstock waste. Cut the step-off marks in to a depth of about 1⁄16 inch.

With the wood well set out, and having checked that your tools are good and sharp, take the parting tool, and sink the narrow band of waste between the base-plug and the bottom of the doll's skirt. Cut in to a depth of about one inch. Next—and still working with the parting tool—lower the spigot or the stepped part of the plug until you finish up with a spigot diameter of about 2⅛ inches.

Toymaking Tip

If you only have a two-inch diameter Forstner bit, or, you are going to gouge out the skirt hollow or whatever, then be sure to modify the cap step to fit.

Once you have established the overall shape and size of the base, or plug, then take the skew chisel and cut away the sharp shoulders to achieve a nice, smooth half-round section to the beading—meaning the part that will finish up as the base of the lady. The best procedure is to divide the thickness of the base into two equal parts by marking the halfway point with a groove, and then to lower and roundover the shoulders at each side of the groove. Having rounded the shoulders, use the parting tool to crisp up the spigot angle (see 2–3). At this point in the project, it's a good idea to refresh your eye by looking at the working drawing and then checking the step-off measurements with the dividers (see 2–4). It's very easy to misread a measurement. My grandpa, with his own style, used to repeat a common aphorism, "If you measure twice and cut once you will get there faster!"

2–3 Use the parting tool to rework the spigot and to take it to a final finish.

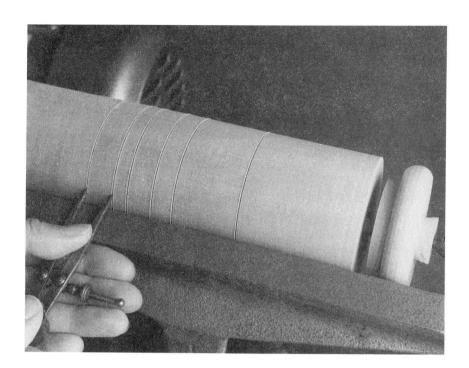

2–4   Double-check the step-off measurements with the dividers.

Finally, with the base cap nicely rounded and stepped—and having used the toe of the skew chisel to make a decorative V-cut around the meridian—take the parting tool, and carefully complete the parting-off cut to separate the plug from the main body of the workpiece.

Woodturning Tip

Although many woodturners lower the speed just before parting off, just as many are happy to part off at speed.

Hollowing and Stepping the Profile

After you have parted the base-plug from the tailstock end of the workpiece, check that the wood is completely secure in the jaws of the chuck, move the tool rest over the bed of the lathe so that you can work the wood end-on, and then true-up the end of the cylinder. That is to say, turn the end to a smooth surface, and make sure that the center point is clearly marked. This done, carefully remove the wood-in-chuck works from the lathe. Being wary that you don't knock or jolt the workpiece in the chuck, move to the bench drill press, and bore out the inside-skirt hollow to a depth of about 1½ inches (see 2–5).

With the skirt cleanly bored out, screw the chuck back on the lathe, cap the hole off with the base-plug, and wind up the tailstock so that the wood is precisely pivoted.

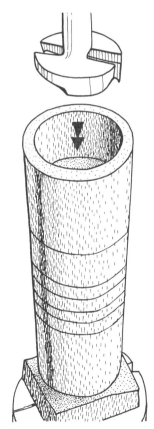

2–5   Use the Forstner bit to bore out the inside-skirt hollow—sink the hole in to a depth of about 1½ inches.

33

Woodturning Tip

You could at this point, if you wish, pop the peas in the cavity and glue-fix the base-plug.

It's important that the wood is well centered, so spend time getting it right. With the wood cleanly centered, take the parting tool and the callipers, and lower all the step-offs to the correct diameters (see 2–6). The skirt needs to be 2½ inches, the top of the body 1½ inches, the neck ½ inch, the face ¾ inch, the hat brim about 1⅛ inches, and the crown of the hat about ⅝ inch. That said, if you want to go for fancier shapes—a round face, or a bigger bodice, or whatever—then this is the time to change the diameters to suit your envisaged design.

Turning the Curved Profile

With the width and depth of all the steps crisply cut, use the round-nosed gouge and/or the skew chisel to turn down all the dips and curves that go to make up the design. Working with the run of the grain, that is, from high to low wood, turn the curve of the hips, the curves at the shoulder and waist, the round face, and so on. And, of course, if along the way you have a notion to modify a curve or add a few extra grooves, or whatever, then be flexible, and let your fancies take over.

FINISHING AND PAINTING

When you have taken the project as far as you want it to go—that is, when you are happy with the overall look of the little figure—use the leather strop to hone the skew chisel to a super-sharp edge. Then set to work skimming the wood down to a fine, smooth finish.

Woodturning Tip

If the skew chisel is sharp, and if you take your time, then you can leave the wood looking so smooth and shiny, that you can leave out the sanding step.

Having turned the wood down to a good finish—and maybe tidied up with a piece of fine-grade sandpaper—use the parting tool and/or the skew chisel to part the wood from the lathe.

Woodturning Tip

When you come to turning the base from the small piece of tailstock waste, undercut the base slightly—with a concavity—to ensure that the finished doll stands firm and square.

2–6 *Reduce the diameter with the parting tool—until the callipers slide over the turning.*

Be extra careful not to make a mess-up at this almost-made-it stage. It's a good idea, to support the whole works—the doll and the plug—just in case the base plug flies loose.

With the workpiece off the lathe, give the parting-off points a quick rub down with the fine-grade sandpaper, and then move to the dust-free area that you have set aside for painting. Study the painting grid (see 2–7).

Start by laying on the large areas of ground color—dark blue for the base-cap and the top of the skirt, light blue for the bodice and the hat crown, white for the band around the hem of the skirt and the hat brim, and pink for the face and neck. When the paint is dry, use the fine-point paintbrush to paint in the details—dark blue buttons and neck ribbon, red cheeks and lips, black hair and face features, and white for the eyes (see 2–8, left). And, of course, once again, if you have a fancy to give the doll a name, a date, or a bit of extra trim, then this is the time.

Having made sure that the acrylic paint is completely dry, give the whole workpiece a couple of coats of varnish, and put it to one side to dry. Finally, when the varnish is good and dry—if you haven't done it earlier—pop a handful of dried peas in the body cavity, and use the Super Glue to attach the base-cap in place (see 2–8, right). The project is ready to hand over to a lucky child.

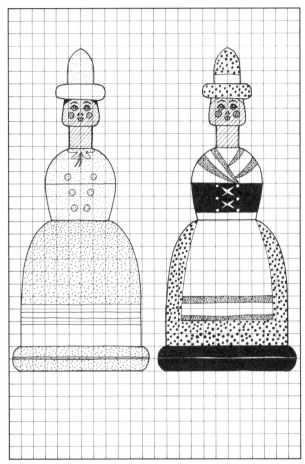

2–8 (Left) After painting the whites of the eyes, use the fine-point paintbrush to paint the pupils and the eye outlines. (Right) Put the noisemakers inside the doll's body and glue-fix the base-plug—if this wasn't done at an earlier stage.

2–7 Painting grid—at a scale of four grid squares to one inch. (Left) The design used in the project. (Right) Alternative design.

TROUBLESHOOTING AND POSSIBLE MODIFICATIONS

- When we came to paint the finished project, we found that the wood—we used jelutong—sucked up the paint. This being so, it might be a good idea, prior to painting, to seal the wood with a thin coat of varnish.
- Watch out for paint/varnish build-up on the plug spigot—it can change a wonderful fit into no fit at all!
- If you decide to use paints other than acrylics, then make sure that they are completely safe and nontoxic. In the context of toys, never be tempted to use leftover domestic paint. I say this, because some household/boat/auto paints do contain toxic materials.
- If you decide to give this shaker a carrying loop—say a hole through the top of the hat and a length of cord—make sure that the loop is small. Long lengths of cord and young children are a bad mix!
- **Never** use odds and ends such as nuts and pins as noisemakers! If a child were curious about what's inside the shaker, and if he/she managed to pry off the base-plug, then it's absolutely critical that the noisemakers found be safe and nontoxic!
- If you are lucky enough to have a tailstock drill chuck, then it's a good idea to bore out the hole while the workpiece is on the lathe.

• 3 •

Jumping Jack

A figure toy with string-operated fly-up arms and legs

Jumping Jack type toys—called *Pantins* in France, *Hampelmann* in Germany, *Zapplemann* in Thuringia, and either Jumping or Merry Jacks in the United States—are little doll-like figures that are characterized by having loosely pivoted limbs and a pull string. When the string is pulled (see 3–1), the little doll throws up its arms and legs as if to say "Isn't life grand! Isn't life fun! Let's jump for joy!"

Just why this traditional toy is still so popular—they have been around at least since the middle of the sixteenth century—I think has something to do with the wonderful directness, naiveté, and undemanding nature of the toy's function. We've watched kids—and adults—playing with jumping jacks, and there is no doubting the feeling of uninhibited pleasure-in-play that comes across. There is something both amusing and hypnotic about the little figures. Up down, up down . . .

For the woodturner, jumping jacks are good fun, a worthwhile challenge to make and put together, a good outlet for using all those odds and ends of wood, and a sure way of turning time into money. If you have a small lathe, if you enjoy working on a small scale, if you like finger-twisting projects that involve lots of little bits and pieces, and if you want to curry favor with all the kids in the neighborhood, then I would say that you are going to enjoy making jumping jacks.

THOUGHTS ON DESIGN AND TECHNIQUE

Have a look at the project picture (see 3–1) and the working drawings (see 3–2). Note how the seven components that go to make up the figure—two boots, two legs, two arms, and a single body-head-and-hat—are turned all-of-a-piece from a single length of wood. That is to say, the single length of wood is mounted on the lathe, and then the component parts are turned like a string of beads. It could be said, that this way of working is wasteful of wood that is removed by turning, but then again, you do get to make seven components at the expense of only two pieces of end waste! Of course, if you prefer, then you could make every component from a separate turning!

The great thing about a project of this character is exactly that it is so flexible. If you want to change the technique, or make the figure a different size, then you can simply adjust the project to suit your needs.

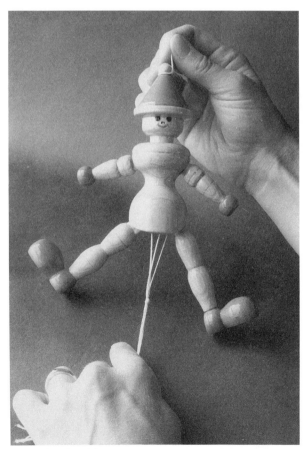

3–1   Project picture.

36

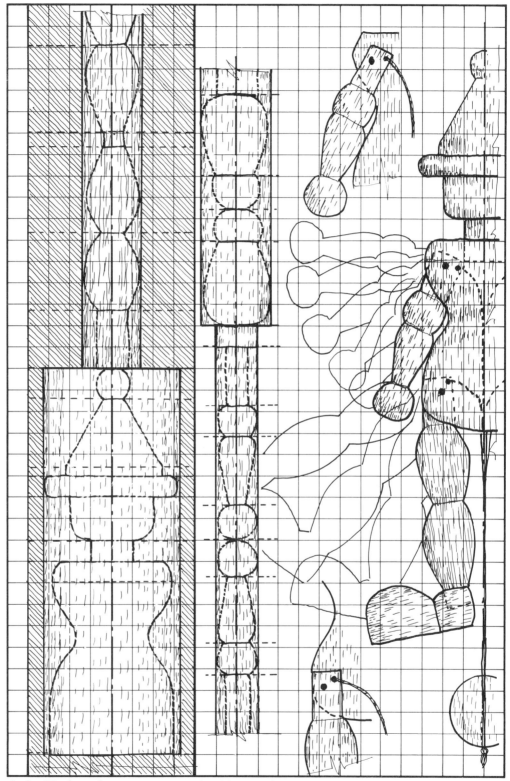

3–2 *Working drawings—at a scale of four grid squares to one inch, the Jumping Jack stands about seven inches high, and five inches wide across the span of outstretched arms. Note the movement of the limbs and the way the joints are pivoted and strung.*

Lathe and Tool Considerations

This project is such that you can, more or less, make it on the lathe of your choice. If you want to turn the limbs on a small power tool lathe as individual spindles between centers, or if, like us, you want to hold the wood in a chuck and turn it all-of-a-piece, then the character of the project allows you to go your own way.

We chose to use an electric scroll saw to cut away the middle-of-body slot because it's just about the swiftest and easiest way of clearing the wood. All you do is mark the slot, run the wood in and out of the saw, and the job is done. Of course, if you don't have the use of a scroll saw, then you are going to have to use a coping saw.

Toymaking Tip

If you enjoy making small toys, then get yourself a scroll saw—they are wonderfully useful machines! We have two machines, a Hegner and a Draper.

Tools and Equipment

Apart from a lathe, you need—
- round-nosed gouge
- parting tool
- skew chisel
- electric scroll saw with a fine blade
- two drill bits—a ¹⁄₁₆-inch twist bit, and a ¹⁄₄-inch Forstner bit
- bench drill press or hand drill
- both dividers and callipers
- pencil and ruler
- sheet each of tracing and workout paper
- small craft knife
- four brass ³⁄₄-inch long panel pins
- pair of pliers
- couple of yards of thin, soft, strong, twine—thin enough to pass through the ¹⁄₁₆-inch diameter holes
- large colored wooden bead—we chose red
- pack of graded sandpapers
- two soft-haired watercolor paintbrushes—a broad and a fine point
- acrylic paints in the colors black and bright red
- small quantity of clear high-gloss varnish
- Super Glue

Wood

For this project you need a 24-inch length of hard, dense-grained wood two by two inches square. Since the main part of the toy is plain varnished, it is best to go for an easy-to-turn wood with an interesting grain. We have chosen a length of white pine, but you could just as well use Southern yellow pine, or just about any easy-to-turn, knot-free wood that comes to hand.

Woodworking Note

Having advised you to avoid knots, you will see from my photographs that I had to work around a hidden knot that suddenly revealed itself at a point about halfway along the length of the wood. Fortunately—after a few minutes spent cursing—I found that I was able to shunt the components along some, and work around the fault.

You don't have to worry too much about this toy being chewed, because, as I see it, it is more a toy for older children. It is also a toy for supervised play such as, you holding, and the kiddy pulling. But always use only nontoxic paints just in case the wrong hands get hold of it.

TOYMAKING STAGES

Setting Out the Wood and First Cuts

When you have a clear understanding of what the project involves, and when you have gathered all your tools and materials and drawn various plans and views up to size, then establish the end center-points by drawing crossed diagonals, and mount the wood securely on the lathe.

As always, make sure that the tool rest is well positioned, turn the wood over by hand, and generally make certain that you and the machine are in good order.

Woodturning Tip

Being mindful that a lathe is potentially a very dangerous machine, it's a good idea to get into the habit of running through a pre-switch-on checklist. Ask yourself—
- Are the tools comfortably at hand, but also not liable to fall onto the lathe?
- Are all your dangling bits—hair, tie, cuffs, jewelry, beard—out of harm's way?
- Are visitors—children, pets, friends—able to watch safely?
- Is the ON/OFF switch fully operational and within easy reach?
- Have you made decisions as to whether or not you are going to wear a mask, goggles, ear protectors, etc.?

When you are happy in the knowledge that all is correct, take the gouge and make several swift passes along the wood—just to make sure that it isn't wildly warped or off-center—and then turn it down to a smooth cylinder.

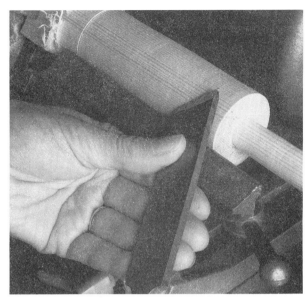

3–3   Use the skew chisel to turn the surface down to a smooth finish. Press the bevel down hard with your thumb.

Aim for the biggest diameter possible. Next, having allowed about 4½ to 5 inches for the body-head-and-hat section, turn the rest of the wood down to a one-inch diameter cylinder. Finally, and this is always a good idea if you are a beginner, use the skew chisel to turn the wood down to a perfect finish (see 3–3). This might seem to be something of a waste of time, because, after all, you are only going to turn the cylinder down to an even smaller diameter, but, then again, it's a great way of getting to know your tools and the wood.

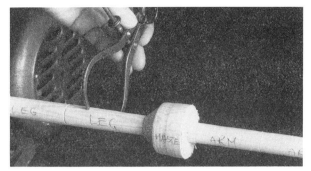

3–5   Double-check the diameters with the callipers.

Setting Out the Steps and Lowering the Waste

When you have realized a cleanly turned cylinder, use the parting tool, dividers, and callipers to step off and lower selected areas. That is to say, set out the length of the various component parts, and turn them down to the required diameter. If you want to copy our cutting order directly—remember, though, that I've had to allow for a knot halfway along the cylinder—take the divider, and, working from left to right along the wood—and having allowed for the body-head-and-hat section—set the one inch diameter cylinder section out with 5½ inches for the two legs, 4½ inches for the two arms, 3 inches for the two boots, and the rest for tailstock waste.

With all the step-offs accurately set out, use the callipers and the tools of your choice to step and lower the various areas of waste (see 3–4). Leaving the body-head-and-hat section be, turn the leg section down to about ¾ inch, the arms down to ½ inch, and the boots down to about ⅞-inch diameter (see 3–5).

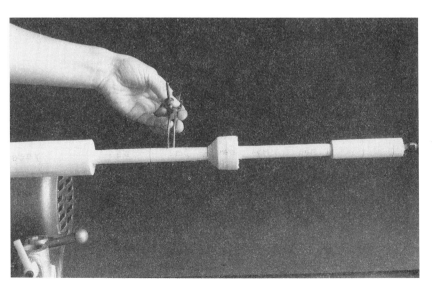

3–4   The primary cylinders.

Of course, just as before, if you intend giving Jack bigger hands, bigger boots, or whatever, then this is the time to modify the diameters. As to your choice of tools, you might use the parting tool for the whole procedure, or, the parting tool to set the diameters and the skew chisel to clear the bulk of the waste, and so forth. I advise you initially to follow what I do, and then, once you know what's what, use the tool and the technique that works for you. Make sure that the end-of-leg spigots—for joining the feet to the boots—are ¼ inch in diameter. Finally, when you are pleased with the various diameters, use the dividers and the skew chisel to set-in and turn all the little V-grooves that fix the position of the high spots of the design (see 3–6, top)—around the chest and around all the swelling muscles of arms and legs.

Woodturning Note

In the context of woodturning, the term "set-in" is the act of using a pencil and/or the divider to mark out the measurements/profiles that go to make up the design.

Turning the Curved Profile

With the width and depth of all the steps crisply cut, then comes the good fun bit of turning down all the shoulders, beads, coves, curves, and tapers that go to make up the design (see 3–6, bottom). So, for example, the hat is made up from a bead, a taper, and a ball; the face is round-shouldered down into the neck; the waist is hollow-curved, or, perhaps, I should say it is coved.

Woodturning Tip

From book to book and woodturner to woodturner, I see that all the dips, hollows, shapes, and profiles have different names. Don't bother worrying about the names and terms, just concentrate on the techniques!

Working with the run of the grain, that is, from high to low wood, use the skew chisel both to cut the guide depths and to shape the various curves. Although just about all the proud convex curves—the shoulders and beads—are best cut with the skew chisel, use the round-nosed gouge for the coved hollows. So, for example, when you come to turning the waist, take the round-nosed gouge, and cut the curve with a careful side-to-center action. Run the gouge down into the dip from one side, and then duplicate and reverse the procedure for the other side. Repeat this procedure several times—one side of the dip and then on the other—until you reach the required depth and profile. Working in this way, you will always be, as it were, working downhill, and so, consequently, approaching and cutting the wood to best advantage.

Continue turning and shaping all the smaller beads, cuts, coves, and curves that go to make up the shape of the legs, arms, and boots.

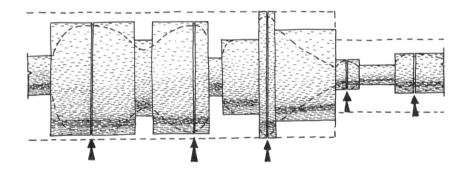

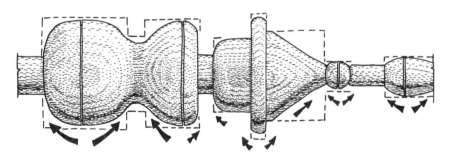

3–6 (Top) Having sunk all the steps that go to make up the design, use the toe of the skew chisel to set-in the V-cuts/ grooves that fix the position of the high spots. (Bottom) Work in the direction of the grain— in the direction of the arrows— from high to low wood.

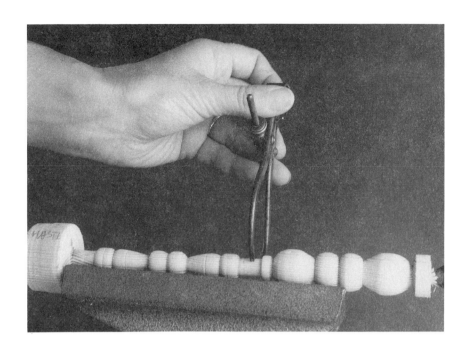

3–7 *Check the various arm and foot diameters before parting off.*

Woodturning Tip

If, along the way, you have a notion to modify a curve, add an extra groove, or whatever, then be flexible, and let your fancies take over. For example, when I came to turning the shape of the boots, I decided to make them as big and as heavy as possible. Be mindful, however, that although it doesn't matter if your shapes and profiles vary from the design, the movement and function of the toy will be best assisted if opposite members are as nearly as possible the same shape and weight. Although you can change the shape of the boots, you still have to ensure that they are as heavy as possible, and a matching pair. In an effort to keep the turnings well balanced and matched, stop every now and again, and check with the calliper that all is correct (see 3–7).

Finally, once you have turned the wood down to the envisaged profile, use the skew chisel and the graded sandpapers to work the wood to a good smooth finish (see 3–8).

Cutting the Limb Slots

When you have turned the bead-like string of shapes, then remove the "string of beads" from the lathe, and use a small saw to cut the turning down into the seven separate component parts. This done, take the body-head-and-hat turning, and pencil label it "front," "back" and "side." Best to have the grain arranged so that the rings are at front and back.

3–8 *Use the heel of the skew chisel to turn the cone shape that goes to make the hat. Work down the slope of the cone.*

When you have clearly labelled the body, use a pencil and ruler to draw a ⅜ inch wide "limb" slot up each side of the figure. Run the slot up from the bottom of the turning, straight on past the chest line and through to the bottom of the neck line. See working drawing details (see 3–2) and look ahead to final photos.

41

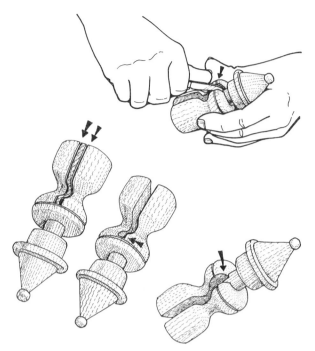

Cutting the Limb Joints and Drilling the Pivot Points

Take the four limbs—the two arms and the two legs—and pencil label them "left" and "right," and "front" and "back," so that you are clear in your own mind how they relate to the figure. Next, use the pencil and ruler to set out the ¼-inch thickness on the side and end faces of the "joint" end of all four limbs. Bearing in mind that you only have one chance to get it right, move to the scroll saw and cut away the waste at either side of the top end of the limbs. Leave the joints flat faced—like tenons. Have a trial fitting of the joints in the body slot, and, as needed, use the knife and sandpaper to adjust the fit. Aim for a nice, easy movement.

Check carefully with both the working drawings (see 3–2) and the actual workpiece in front of you to see how the limbs need to pivot and swing in a clear uninterrupted arc. This done, use the ¹⁄₁₆-inch diameter bit, to bore out all the pivot, pin, and string holes—through the limb joints and through the body (see 3–10 and 3–11). When you are drilling the limb holes, support them on a piece of scrap to prevent the wood from splitting as the drill exits. Run the body holes in from the back of the body, stopping short at the slot.

Toymaking Note

As far as I can see, there's no easy way of fixing the position of the through-body holes, other than doing it by eye. Best of luck with this bit!

3–9 (Bottom left) Run two parallel cuts from the bottom of the figure to stop short at the little V-cut that marks out the position of the high point around the chest. Link the cuts at the shoulders so that the waste falls away. (Top and bottom, right) Use the knife to slice away the small piece of waste between the chest line and the neck.

Having shaded in the "limb" slot so that there is no doubting its position, move to the scroll saw and set to work clearing the slot. First, run two cuts from the bottom of the figure to stop short at the little V-cut that marks out the high point of the chest (see 3–9, bottom left). Aim to set the cuts a little to the waste side of the drawn line. Link the two parallel cuts so that the slice of waste falls clear. Take the knife, and whittle away at the shoulder area—meaning between the chest line and the bottom of the neck—to sink the slot in as far as the side of the neck. Do this on both sides of the figure (see 3–9, top right). Use the saw, knife, and sandpaper to cut away the bottom of the slots so that the body runs in a smooth curve from the bottom to the side.

Finally, shape and fit the two boots. Use the knife to slice away the roundness on one side of each boot turning, and then rub the knife-worked face down to a good finish. Strive to achieve two well-matched boots. With the boots accurately shaped, mark the top center points, and then sink a ¼-inch diameter hole about ⅛-inch down into the wood. Glue the legs into the holes, and put them to one side until the glue is set.

3–10 Back view—the five component parts ready to be painted. Note the various pivot and string holes.
3–11 Side view—note the limb slot.

FINISHING, PAINTING, AND PUTTING TOGETHER

Once you have cut the slots and limb joints, drilled all the pin, pivot, and string holes, then comes the amazingly pleasurable and rewarding task of finishing and putting the toy together. Having glue-fitted the boots in place, have a trial fitting of the limbs. That is, slot the limbs in place, push the pins through the pivot holes, and generally see that the limbs swing free.

When, by means of some amount of patient endeavor—sanding, slicing, and whatever it takes—you have achieved a good easy swing of the arms and legs, wipe away the dust and debris, and move to the clean and tidy dust-free area that you have set aside for painting. Have a look at the painting grid (see 3–12). Paint the hands, hat, mouth, and boots bright red, and the nose and eye dots black. Wait for the acrylic paint to dry, and then give the whole toy a couple of coats of clear high-gloss varnish. Put it to one side to dry.

Have another look at the working drawings (see 3–2)—just so that you know what goes where. Use a pin to clear out the pivot holes, knot about 12 inches of fine cord to each limb end, position and pin the limbs in place in the body slot, gather all the cords together, knot on the bead, tie a cord to Jumping Jack's hat bobble, and . . . "Yippee—isn't life grand!" the toy is ready to go.

TROUBLESHOOTING AND POSSIBLE MODIFICATIONS

- There is no problem, if you decide to change the shape of the toy, as long as you make sure that the hands and boots are heavy enough to pull the limbs down to the at-rest position.
- In retrospect, I would have made the hands much larger and heavier—like the boots. The added weight makes for a more positive and pleasing movement.
- If you are at all worried about the problem of how to fix the precise position of the pivot points—in the

3–12   Painting grid. (Left) The painted design as used in this project. (Right) Alternative design.

limbs and the body—then make a quick mock-up out of rough wood, and have several trial-and-error attempts.
- If you think that there's a chance that you are going to make a mess-up with fitting the limbs, then it might be just as well to turn off a few spare sets, to be on the safe side.

• 4 •

Baby's Rattle with Rings

A rattle with three captive rings—turned all-of-a-piece from a single length of wood

Kids like rattles! There is something really exciting about a hold-in-the-hand toy that can be clicked and clattered, tipped and tapped, and generally shaken around (see 4–1). It's good fun!

Beginners to woodturning tend to be intrigued and somewhat baffled about the notion of turning an item with one or more captive rings. The big question is how is it done? Well, the rings aren't made individually and then broken and glued in place, nor are they slid onto a separately turned spindle. Nothing so complicated! The answer is simple and direct; the rings and the spindle—the whole works—are turned all-of-a-piece from a single length of wood. This is achieved by means of the skillful, not to say tricky, use of the skew chisel and/or a special hook-shaped scraper.

And is it easy? Like most turning techniques, it's pretty straightforward when you know how. You might make a mess-up the first time around, but you should get it right after a few trial-and-error attempts.

If you are looking to expand your turning skills, and if you know of a baby who could use a rattle, then I would say that this is the project for you.

DESIGN AND TECHNIQUE BASICS

Once you have decided to make the project, it's always a good idea to do a bit of background research. To this end, you might look at museums and folk art collections, visit craft shops, flip through old books and magazines, and so on. Study traditional captive-ring turnings that were made in the past—rattles, goblets with rings around the stem, and such.

Woodturning Tip

If you enjoy turning, then it's always a good idea to take a sketchbook on your museum or gallery visits.

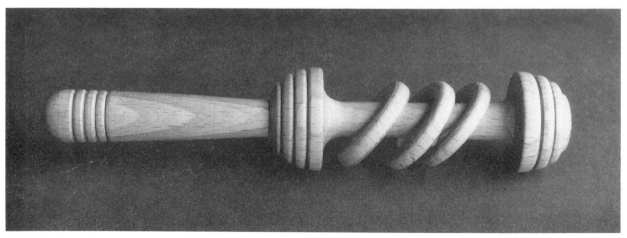

4–1 *Project picture.*

When you have a clear picture in your mind's eye of the possibilities, and how you want the project to be, have a good, long look at the project picture (see 4–1), and the details of the working drawings (see 4–2). Note how—on the working drawings—there is a ½-inch space between neighboring rings as well as between the rings and the half-bead body of the rattle. Be mindful that the ½-inch spacing is the minimum space needed for the manipulation of the turning ring-cutting tool. This being so, if you decide to make a much larger rattle, or maybe use the technique to make curtain rings, rings on the ends of a rolling pin, or whatever, then make sure that you still allow ½-inch between neighboring rings, and between the first/last rings in line and the body of the turning.

Note how the central spindle profile runs in a smooth curve up to the flat face of the body. Consider how we have given the rattle a few fancy details by running decorative beading rings around the domed ends and around the handle.

Lathe and Tool Considerations

I favor using a four-jaw chuck, because I can take the project more or less to completion before drawing the tailstock back out of the way, finishing off the tailstock end of the turning, and then parting off. Although I use the four-jaw chuck for most projects, this is not to say that you can't work with the wood held between centers—meaning between the pronged headstock and the tailstock centers.

Woodturning Tip

If you do use a four-jaw chuck, be careful that the spinning jaws don't catch your hand. Build a guard or cover to shield the chuck.

If however you do decide to work between centers, then the best procedure is to take the work almost to completion, remove the workpiece from the lathe, and then use a

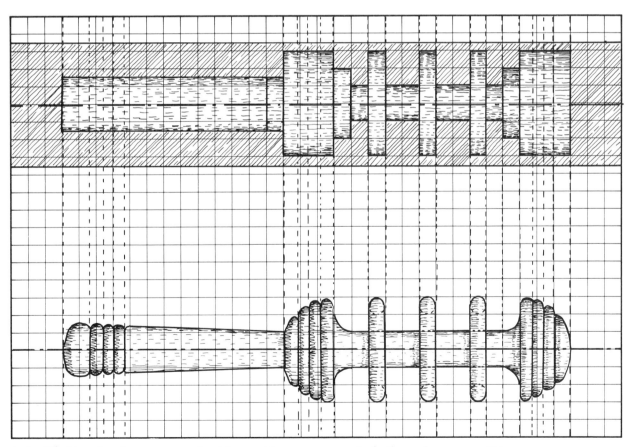

4–2 *Working drawings—at a scale of four grid squares to one inch, the rattle measures 7½ inches in total length, and 1½ inches across the diameter of the rings.*

fine-bladed saw to cut away the head and tailstock waste. If you do decide to go for this option, then leave at least ½ inch for tailstock waste.

As for your choice of tools, the only real point of discussion in this project, is whether or not to use a skew chisel or a special hooked tool for cutting the rings. Ask yourself whether you are going to make captive rings in future projects? If you are, then you might as well invest in an easy-to-use hooked tool.

Tools and Equipment

Apart from a lathe, you need—
- round-nosed gouge
- parting tool
- skew chisel
- double-sided captive-ring scraper
- small round-nosed scraper
- both dividers and callipers
- pencil and ruler
- sheet each of tracing and workout paper
- pack of graded sandpapers

Wood

For this project you need a 10-inch length of hard, dense-grained wood at 1¾ inch by 1¾ inch square. We've chosen beech, but you could just as well select a wood like box or cherry. The main thing to bear in mind, of course, when you are choosing your wood, is that the rattle is likely to be sucked and chewed by the child. This being so, the wood must be splinter resistant, colorfast, and nontoxic.

In the context of toys, and as a general rule of thumb, I think it is best to avoid exotic woods. I say this, because one or two rare dark woods have been proved to be allergenic. Prolonged wet-skin contact—when, for example, a child is sucking a toy—can produce an allergic reaction. If you have any doubts, ask your supplier.

TOYMAKING STAGES

Mounting the Wood on the Lathe and First Steps

After you have gathered together all your tools and materials, and drawn and traced the design at full size, take your 10-inch length of wood and give it a last swift check over—just to make sure that it's free from nasties such as loose knots and splits. When you are happy with the wood, establish the end centers by drawing crossed diagonals, and then mount the wood securely on the lathe. There is no problem if you decide to use a four-jaw chuck and a live tailstock center—all you do is draw up

the tailstock and tighten up the chuck. If, on the other hand, you are using a fork center with a dead center, fix the wood between centers, wind the tailstock up to drive the center into the wood, and then ease back the tailstock slightly, dribbling a drop or two of oil on the point of spin.

With the wood nicely secured, bring the tool rest up to the work, turn the wood over by hand—just to make sure it's not touching—and then tighten up.

With the wood in place, switch on the power and get to work. Take a gouge—either square or round nosed—and make several passes along the wood. Clear away the bulk of the rough, and turn the wood to a nice smooth 1½-inch (or thereabouts) diameter cylinder.

Setting Out the Design and Sinking the Waste

When you have achieved a crisp cylinder—it can be slightly bigger or smaller than 1½ inch in diameter—then use the dividers to transfer the primary measurements from the tracing to the workpiece (see 4–3). So, for example, if we take it that the rattle handle is at the headstock end of the workpiece, make step-offs from left to right along the workpiece 1¼ inches for headstock waste, 3¼ inches for the handle, ¾ inch for the first half-bead, ½ inch for waste, ¼ inch for the first ring, ½ inch for waste, ¼ inch for the second ring, ½ inch for waste, ¼ inch for the third ring, ¾ inch for the half-bead at the top end of the rattle, and a final small amount for tailstock waste.

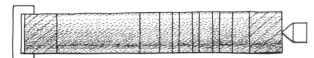

4–3 Turn the 1½-inch-diameter cylinder, and use the dividers to step-off all of the measurements that go to make up the design.

Woodturning Note

As you can see from the photos, the tailstock waste split off at a very early stage. Although I was more than a bit peeved—as you might guess—but as the rest of the wood looked sound, I decided to carry on and try to include the resultant cone-shaped depression into the design.

If by chance you do make a mess-up at some point along the way—with this or any project—then it's always worth trying to modify your work to incorporate the fault or problem into the design!

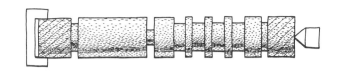

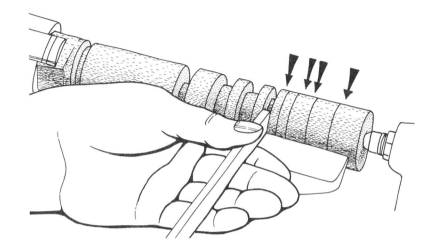

4–4 Take the parting tool and sink a ¼-inch wide, ¼-inch deep trench on either side of all three rings. Define the waste at the end of the rattle.

Having carefully noted that there are four ½-inch bands of waste in all, take the parting tool, and sink a ¼-inch wide, ½-inch deep trench on either side of all three rings (see 4–4). If all goes well, the side-by-side sinkings between the first and second ring, and between the second and third ring, should join to make ½-inch wide channels at either side of the middle ring.

Finally, still working with the parting tool, sink pilot channels to establish the diameters at either end of the tapered handle.

Turning the Profile

When you have used the parting tool to establish the width of the three rings and the diameter at either end of the handle, then comes the very satisfying task of generally shaping the form. Have a good, long look at the working drawing (see 4–2)—just so that you are clear in your own mind as to how the various profiles relate to one another—then use the skew chisel and the round nosed gouge to clear the waste and define the shape of the rattle. Using the gouge, work along the handle—from the end and towards the middle—and partially turn the shape of the taper. Then, use the skew chisel to round-over and cut-in the half-ball—or you might say half-bead—curves at either end of the ring section (see 4–5). Hold the chisel at an angle so that the heel does the work. As needed, slow the lathe down, and raise the height of the rest so that the chisel is cutting the wood from above.

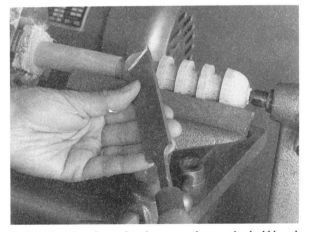

4–5 Use the skew chisel to round-over the half-bead curves at either end of the ring section.

Woodturning Tip

If you are a beginner, have a practice try-out with the skew chisel before you start the project. It's a wonderfully efficient tool, but only when you know how!

Be mindful as you are working, that the most efficient cut is one that runs in the direction of the grain, that is, from high to low wood—from a peak down into a valley. In the context of the rattle, you would cut from the end of the handle in towards the body, and from high point of

47

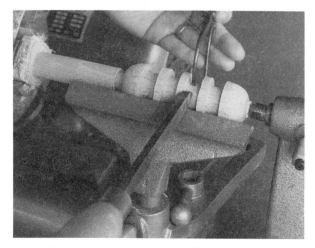

4–6 *Use the parting tool and callipers to precisely cut and measure the between-ring channels.*

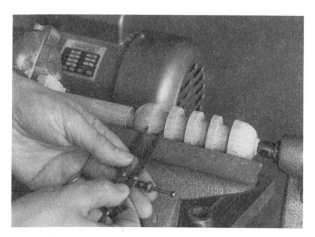

4–7 *Check the between-ring channels with the dividers.*

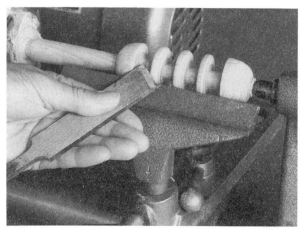

4–8 *Use the skew chisel to round the outer curves or shoulders of the rings.*

the half-bead top of the rattle down towards the head-stock, and so on. Don't be in too much of a hurry, and don't apply too much pressure.

When you are happy with the overall shape and finish, use the parting tool to further define and refine the width and depth of the channels, and the width of the rings. Use the dividers and callipers to double-check measurements (see 4–6 and 4–7).

Finally, when you have achieved what you consider is a good sound shape, then resharpen the chisel, and take the handle and the dome-ends to a smooth finish.

Cutting the Captive Rings

Once you have generally turned the body and the handle of the rattle to a good shape and finish, then comes the testing, or you might say proving, make-or-break task of turning the rings. Start by sinking the between-ring channels to the finished depth of ½ inch so that the spindle measures ½-inch in diameter. Next, use the skew chisel to turn the sharp edges off the rings to give them a nice rounded or beaded section (see 4–8). If you are a bit worried about using the heel of the chisel on such a slender section, then use it flat-down like a scraper.

With the three rings nicely turned and rounded, take the round-nosed scraper and repeat the channel-sinking procedure before the first ring and after the third ring to run the line of the spindle up in a smooth curve through to the body (see 4–9).

Take the hooked scraper, and, starting at the first ring along from the headstock, angle the tip of the tool into the first channel so that it's touching the blank face of the ring at a point about ⅜ inch in from the outer edge, and start to cut the ring section on the side-face of the ring blank.

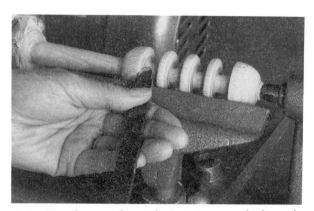

4–9 *Use the round-nosed scraper to run the line of the spindle up in a smooth radius curve to the large half-ball detail. Do this at both ends.*

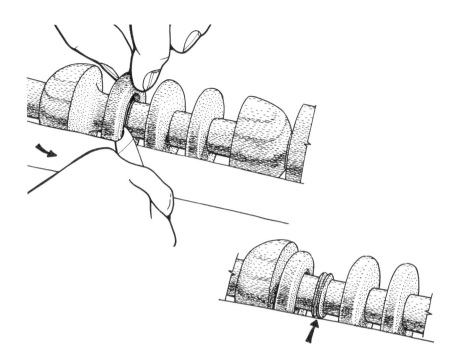

4–10 (Top) Support the ring with your thumb and index finger, and use the hooked tool to undercut, shape, and part off. (Bottom) Use the tool of your choice to turn the small piece of waste off the spindle.

Continue cutting the groove on one side of the ring blank, and then onto the other, until gradually you cut and define the shape of the ring. When you have almost cut through the ring, ease off the pressure slightly, support the ring between thumb and index finger, and then complete the cut so that the ring spins free (see 4–10, top). When you have cut the first ring, take the parting tool, and with the ring held to one side, carefully clear the small amount of inside-ring waste from around the spindle (see 4–10, bottom).

And, of course, when you have turned and cleared one ring, you repeat the procedure for the other two. It's all pretty straightforward, the only real difficulty is how to hold the rings out of the way when you are clearing the waste from around the spindle. Don't—like me—be tempted to tape the rings together or tape the rings to the central spindle. When I experimented with variously taping and tying the rings out of the way, all that happened was that they built up an off balance momentum, and generally threatened to rip the workpiece off the lathe and tangle up with the turning tools. Very dramatic—but not a good idea!

FINISHING

Having turned the three rings, take the skew chisel and cut in all the little decorative beads that go to make up the design—around the end of the handle, and at either side of the main body. Use the toe of the skew chisel to set-in the position of the beads with V-cuts (see 4–11, top).

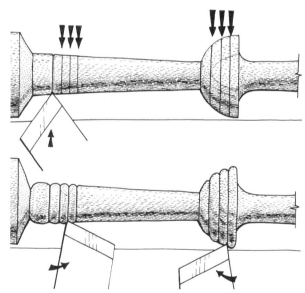

4–11 (Top) Use the toe of the skew chisel to establish the V-cuts that define the decorative beads. (Bottom) Turn the beads to shape with the toe of the skew chisel—like a scraper.

With the guidelines cut in, use the toe of the chisel as you would use a scraper, and turn the beads to shape (see 4–11, bottom). Define the beads so that they reflect the shape of the captive rings. Take it slowly at this stage so that you do not knock the workpiece off center.

Bearing in mind that the rattle is almost certainly going to be sucked and chewed, take the finest grade of sandpaper and rub the whole works down to a super-smooth finish. Make sure that it's absolutely free from splinters and rough edges.

Finally, part the rattle off from the lathe, rub the part-off points down with the fine sandpaper, and give the rattle to a child!

TROUBLESHOOTING AND POSSIBLE MODIFICATIONS

- If you are working on a very small lathe, then it's a good idea to clear away some of the waste before mounting the workpiece on the lathe. All you do is establish the end centers by drawing crossed diagonals, scribe circles out on the ends of the wood, draw tangents at the circle-diagonal cross-over points, draw lines from the resultant octagons to establish the along-the-wood waste, and then clear the waste with a rasp or plane.
- If you are at all worried about the project, then it's always a good idea to have a try-out on a piece of scrap wood. That said, don't use a piece of rough knotty pine and expect good results!
- If you decide to use a skew chisel for cutting the rings— rather than a hooked tool, it's also a good idea to have a pre-project try-out.
- If you are concerned that your child might chew and break the rings, then consider making the rings somewhat thicker.
- As the rattle is going to be chewed/sucked, it is best not to wax the finished project. If, however, you want to give the wood a dribble-proof finish, then give it a wipe over with vegetable cooking oil, or maybe seal it with a thin matt varnish.
- If you want to make a fancier, noisier rattle, then you could turn a series of grooves or beads along the central spindle so that the rings click along the rippled surface.

•5•

Dutch Doll with Jointed Limbs

A doll with joints at the shoulders, elbows, hips, and knees

Simple wooden folk art dolls—known variously as, peg dolls, German dolls, Dutch or Deutsch dolls, and Bohemian dolls—are characterized by being made of wood, being turned and/or carved, having movable joints, and by being painted with simple stylized imagery (see 5–1).

In Europe, turned wooden Dutch dolls of this type—worked traditionally as a cottage industry—were turned, carved, jointed, and painted in the winter, sold in job lots to buyers or middle men in the spring, sold on to shops and exporters, and then finally graded and sold as sets or families to the doll-buying public.

The wonderfully reassuring thing is that, even after two world wars, all manner of oppressive political regimes, the introduction of plastics, and all the other dramatic upsets and changes that have occurred in, say, the last seventy years, countries such as the Czech Republic, Hungary, Poland, and Germany, are still making "Dutch" dolls, much as they were in the nineteenth century.

Traditionally, the dolls were given a simple painted blouse, and sold in their "undressed" state, the idea being, that the purchaser would make the doll a set of proper clothes. If you enjoy turning, and if you know of a child who needs a doll, and maybe a parent who likes making doll's clothes, then this is a choice project.

DESIGN AND TECHNIQUE BASICS

When you have gathered together all your tools and materials, take a trip to the nearest folk museum, and look for wooden folk art dolls that were made in Europe and the United States in the nineteenth century. Ask especially to see so-called "Dutch" dolls. Note how different systems are used for the movable joints. For example, some have small ball joints, others are hinged with string and/or leather, and yet others—like our doll—

have tongue-and-groove type joints that are pivoted with wood pins.

Have a look at our project picture (see 5–1) and the working drawings (see 5–2 and 5–3), and note the way that the elements are first turned, and then modified by being variously trimmed and whittled to shape. For example, the lower part of the body is flattened at the back, front, and sides for the hips, and then reduced at either side of the upper body, for the arms.

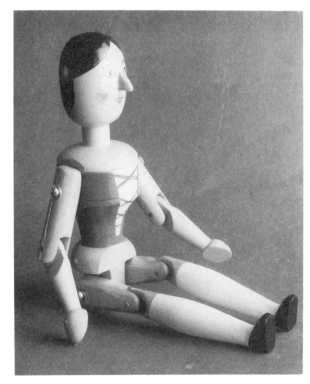

5–1   Project picture.

Consider also, the way that the shoulder and hip joints are pivoted with brass roundhead screws, while the elbows and knees are fitted with wooden pins. Note especially, the way that the feet are first turned so that they have a mushroom-like form, and then are trimmed at the back and sides to create the characteristic feet. Continue studying all the details, until you have a crystal clear understanding of just how the doll needs to be made and put together. And, of course, if you have in mind making the doll bigger or smaller, going for more sophisticated joints, or whatever, then this is the time to modify the design accordingly.

Lathe and Tool Considerations

Although, as always, we have chosen to use a four-jaw chuck, this is one of those beautifully flexible projects that can easily be worked between centers. The chuck does allow for the head to be taken to completion before the workpiece is taken from the lathe, but aside from that, the project can be worked as a group of between-center spindles.

We have used a sanding disc to rub down the flat faces that go to make the design—the mating fit of the arms to the body, the flat areas at the hips, and the hands. It's a wonderfully swift operation, but be mindful that a lathe sander produces a huge amount of dust. If you are going to use a sander, then be sure to wear a pair of goggles and a dust mask, or, better still, a wrap-around hat-and-mask-type respirator.

Tools and Equipment

Apart from a lathe, you need—
• round-nosed gouge

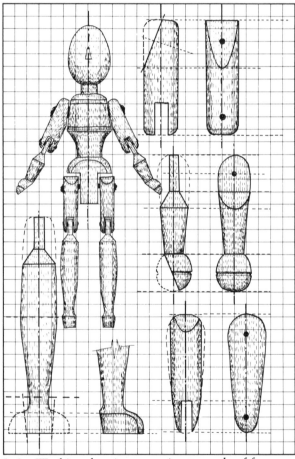

5–2 Working drawings—at a scale of four grid squares to one inch, the doll stands about 12 inches high and is three inches wide across the span of the shoulders. Note how, in side view, the hips have been reduced and shaped.

5–3 Working drawings—again at a scale of four grid squares to one inch for the limbs—but at two grid squares to one inch for the complete inset drawing. Note how the initial turnings need to be rubbed down to make the joints, hands, and shoes.

- parting tool
- skew chisel
- both dividers and callipers
- pencil and ruler
- sheet each of tracing and workout paper
- pack of graded sandpapers
- coping saw with a fine blade
- penknife
- four roundhead brass screws about one inch long
- sixteen small brass washers to fit the screws
- bench drill press with a selection of fine bits
- six-inch length of ⅛-inch dowel
- acrylic paints in the colors beige pink, white, dark blue, black, and red
- Super Glue

Wood

For this project you need a 10-inch length of lightweight easy-to-turn wood 2½ by 2½ inches square for the body, a 16-inch length of wood 1½ by 1½ inches square for the four elements that go to make up the legs, and a 12½-inch length of wood one by one inch square for the parts that go to make the arms.

TOYMAKING STAGES

The Body—Mounting the Wood on the Lathe and First Cuts

Having studied the working drawings (see 5–2 and 5–3), and drawn the designs at full size, take the 10-inch length of wood—the piece for the body—establish the end centers by drawing crossed diagonals, and mount it securely on the lathe. Run through your pre-switch-on checklist—see that the lathe is in good, safe order—and switch on the power. Take the large gouge, and swiftly cut away the rough, turning the wood down to a cylindrical section. Aim, at first, for the largest possible diameter.

When you have achieved a round section, take the skew chisel and the callipers, and carefully turn the wood down to a smooth two-inch diameter.

Woodturning Tip

Although it's easy enough to turn the cylinder to a finished measurement with the gouge, we prefer to go for a swift gouge-turned cylinder—one that is well oversize—and then use the skew to skim down to a good finish. We have developed the habit of using this stage to fine-tune skew chisel skills.

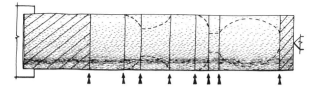

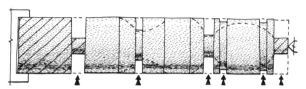

5–4 (Top) Mark in all the step-offs that go to make the design of the body. (Bottom) Use the parting tool and the callipers to set in all the pilot and parting cuts.

Having achieved what you consider is a good two-inch diameter cylinder, take the ruler and dividers, and mark out all the step-offs that go to make the design of the body (see 5–4, top). With the head end being nearest to the tailstock, allow ½ inch for tailstock waste, 2¼ inches for the head, about ⅜ inch for the neck, ½ inch for the shoulders, one inch for the chest, 1⅛ inch for the waist, ⅝ inch for the curve of the hips, 1¼ inches for the hips, and the remainder for waste.

Woodturning Tip

If you are working between centers—without a chuck—then allow extra wood at the tailstock.

With the step-offs in place, take the parting tool and the calliper, and begin the pilot cuts (see 5–4, bottom). Sink two ⅛-inch deep cuts for the head, two side-by-side ⅝-inch deep cuts for the neck, and a single, ½-inch deep cut for the waist. Aim to leave the various core diameters slightly larger than the finished diameter. So, for example, if we take it that you are starting out with a two-inch diameter cylinder, the two ⅛-deep cuts on the head will leave you with a 1¾-inch diameter head, which is just a skim larger than the finished diameter. With the guide cuts in place, use the tool of your choice to lower the waste. Finally, take the parting tool, and sink the waste at the head and hips.

Woodturning Tip

We always rehone the parting tool just prior to parting off. The time taken not only means that the tool will be cutting to best effect, but it gives you a breather before the final parting off.

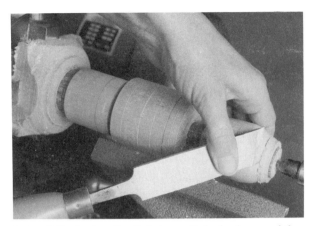

5–5 *Lift the handle slightly until the heel part of the blade begins to bite, and then advance the cut in a smooth sweeping-and-lifting movement. Use the same procedure to lower the waste.*

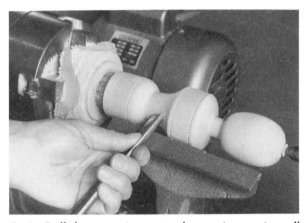

5–6 *Roll the gouge in a smooth scooping motion, all the while making sure that the bevel is leaning hard-in on the wood.*

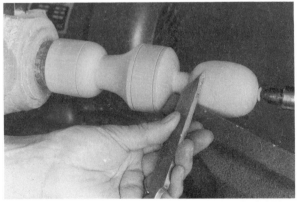

5–7 *Use the toe of the skew chisel to clean out the sharp angles at the neck.*

Shaping the Profile

Take the dividers, and divide the 2¼ inch long head into two equal halves. Don't make the mark too deep—just a scratch to indicate the high point. This done, take the skew chisel, and set to work turning the egg-like head to shape (see 5–5). The procedure is to set the chisel flat down on the high spot—so that the heel end of the cutting edge is "looking towards" the direction of the cut—lift the handle slightly until the heel of the blade begins to bite, and then advance-sweep-and-lift in a continuous smooth movement to lower the waste.

If you are doing it right, the waste will come off as a shaving, and the heel of the blade will finish up in the valley. And so proceed, repeatedly making passes, until you have turned down the half-egg shape and the blade is sitting in the valley in the vertical position. And, of course, when you have completed one-half of the egg-shaped head, all you do is turn the tool over so that the blade is "looking" in the other direction, and repeat the procedure as already described.

When you have finished the head, then continue with the skew chisel, and use much the same procedure, to turn the shape of the rounded bead or shoulder that runs down from the chest into the neck as well as the round shape of the hips.

Woodturning Tip

If you are at all worried about this procedure, and perhaps find that the toe of the chisel catches as it runs around the curve, then set the chisel flat-down on the tool rest, and use the toe to scrape the profile to shape. Certainly this way of working tends to take the edge off the tool, and it might be considered to be a bit sloppy, but, then again, it's a swift, easy way of working, you don't have to select another tool, and it gets the job done.

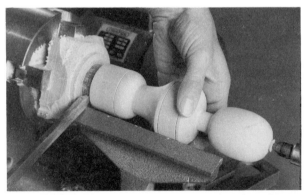

5–8 *Support the workpiece with one hand, and part-off from the lathe.*

When you are ready to turn the tapered curve that runs down from the chest to the waist, take the round-nosed gouge, set it side-down on the high spot—so that the inside of the gouge is "looking towards" the waste that needs to be cut away, and then roll the gouge in a smooth scooping motion, all the while making sure that the bevel leans in on the wood (see 5–6). Make a series of small cuts with the small area of the blade just below the midpoint. If you are doing it right, by the time you reach the bottom of the taper or cove, then the gouge should more or less be sitting at rest on its back.

Use the toe of the skew to cut-in the decorative grooves on the chest and to clean out the sharp angles at the waist and neck (see 5–7). Finally, give the whole workpiece a swift rub down with the fine grade sandpaper, and part it off from the lathe (see 5–8).

Turning the Arms

Take the 12½-inch length of one-by-one inch section—the piece for the arms—fix the position of the end center points by drawing crossed diagonals, and mount it securely on the lathe. Start by using first the gouge and the skew chisel to turn the wood to a smooth diameter of about ¾ inch. Don't worry too much if it's slightly larger

than ¾ inch. This done, study the working drawings (see 5–3), refresh your eye, and then take the divider, and working from left to right along the workpiece—that is, from the headstock end—allow about 1½ inches for chuck waste, two inches for one forearm, ¾ inch for one hand, ¾ inch for the other hand, two inches for the other forearm, 2¼ inches for one upper arm, 2¼ inches for the other upper arm, and the rest for tailstock waste. Note how the two lower arms are arranged so that the two hands are together (see 5–9, top).

With all the primary step-offs carefully set out, continue with the divider, and set out the main guidelines. Halve each of the two ¾-inch hands—to mark the high spot—make a mark about 1⅛ inches down from the top end of the forearm, and so on. If you think that such and such a procedure is going to be easier to turn if there are guidelines, then this is the time to set them out.

When all the step-offs and guidelines are in place, take the skew chisel, and set-in the main divisions. Working with the toe, first make V-cuts so that each component is clearly defined, then follow through by sinking a ⅛-inch deep V-cut around the line of the wrist (see 5–9, bottom). Next, still working with the skew chisel, start to turn all the shapes and profiles that go to make up the design.

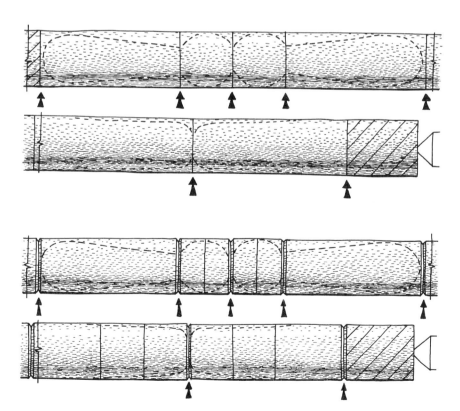

5–9 Note that turning is shown in two halves. (Top) Set out all the primary step-offs that go to make the design. (Bottom) Having made V-cuts to clearly define the component parts, establish the line of the wrist.

55

The procedure is much the same as with the body in that the form is made up from beads or half-balls, slow tapers, and round shoulders. So, for example, the hands are turned as balls and the forearms as tapers. That said, since the wood is thinner and the scale smaller, there is a danger that the wood will bow and split. It's a good idea not only to be more cautious, but also to support the wood while it is being worked. The key word is "support." For example, when you come to turning the tapered forearms, the best procedure is to hold and control the chisel and the wood with one hand, while guiding the tool with the other. Meaning—set the skew chisel flat-down on the workpiece, and cradle the wood with your fingers, while at the same time pressing down on the chisel with your thumb. Working in this way, you will be able to control the bowing of the wood by squeezing the tool and the wood together between thumb and finger.

Complete the turning by carefully skimming the tool over the surfaces to remove the ridges. Use the toe of the chisel to tidy up between each component (see 5–10). Cut the midline on the hands by turning the tool on edge (see 5–11).

Finally, once you have made four nicely turned components, give them a swift rub down with sandpaper, and remove the whole workpiece from the lathe. Note that at a later stage the components are sawn apart.

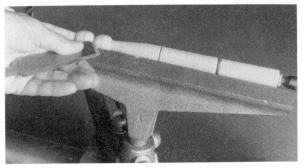

5–10   Use the toe of the skew—like a scraper—to clean up the join line between the components.

Turning the Legs

Start by mounting the wood on the lathe and turning it down to a smooth 1¼-inch diameter cylinder. Note that, although the legs are turned in much the same way as the arms, the procedure is slightly tricky in that the legs have a much more defined shape. That is to say, since beautifully shaped legs characterize the doll—the swell of the calf running smoothly into a long taper and the slender ankle mushrooming into the foot—there is all the more reason for the turning to be carefully managed. The shape has to be just right, not too fat nor too thin, but just so.

Take the divider, and working from left to right along the cylinder, set out the step-offs—a small amount for chuck waste, 4⅜ inches for the first lower leg and foot, 4⅜ inches for the second lower leg and foot, 2½ inches for the first thigh, 2½ inches for the second thigh, and the remainder for waste. This done, continue with the divider and mark out the secondary guidelines at the swell of the calf and at the ankle. Allow about ¾ inch for the foot—refer to the working drawing (see 5–3). Having set in all the step-offs with the divider, sink a single ½-inch deep guide cut—one on each leg—at about ¾ inch up from the bottom of the foot.

With all the guide marks in place, take first the round-nosed gouge and then the skew chisel, and clear away the bulk of the rough. Use the skew chisel to tidy up the step between the foot and the ankle (see 5–12). This done, start the delicate task of turning the limbs to shape. Start it nice and easy, working from the high spots down into the valleys. Every three or four cuts, take the callipers and check the turning against the working drawings. When you come to working the ankle, treat it in much the same way as you would an urn or taper. That is, work from the foot down to the ankle, from the calf down to the ankle, and so on, until you have turned the delicate curve that runs from the foot to the calf. Along the way, you have to keep adjusting one or the other of the legs until you have a nicely matched pair (see 5–13).

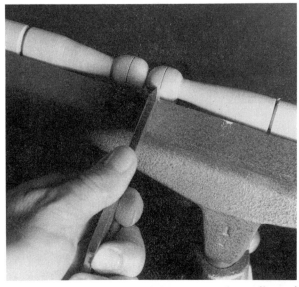

5–11   Use the toe of the skew to cut-in the midline of the hands.

Finally, once you have achieved the four parts that go to make up the two legs, rub them down with the fine-grade sandpaper, and take the turning from the lathe.

Sanding and Sawing

Start by using the saw to cut limb turnings into their component parts. Take the single, large body-head component, and pencil mark the "front" and "back." Now, study the working drawings again (see 5–2), and see how the turning needs to be flattened off at front and back at the hips, and at either side of the chest for the arms. Take the workpiece to the sanding disc and reduce the wood accordingly. Begin sanding nice and easy—little by little—until the arm flats are angled back towards the shoulders, and the hip block is tapered in side view, from a maximum thickness of about one inch at the top of the hips to about ¾ inch at the tail. Once again, the secret is to go at it very gradually, all the while checking your progress against the working drawings.

Take the lower legs, and sand down the mushroom-like foot turning at the back and sides—refer to the working drawings (see 5–3, bottom left)—to create the characteristic foot shape. Try and arrange the foot so that the grain runs from the back of the heel to the toes. Last but not least, sand down the upper arms so that they angle out from the body, the thighs so that they sit flush, and the inside face of the hands to make the "palms."

Having established all the flat surfaces on the sander, then comes the difficult task of cutting all the joints. Start by pencil marking the joints "front" and "back," and drawing in the tongue-and-groove shapes (see 5–14). Divide the thickness of the wood—on the limbs and at the hips—into thirds. This done, very carefully shade in all the areas that need to be cut away—inside the groove on the upper arms and thighs, at either side of the tongues on the top of the lower legs and lower arms, and at either side of the hips. Now, having first made several checks that you have it right, use the coping saw to cut away the waste.

Finally, wrap a small piece of sandpaper around a slender stick, and sand all the joints to a smooth finish and a good fit.

A Trial Putting Together

After you have again studied the working drawings (see 5–3) to see how the various joints are placed and pivoted, mark all the pivot points by eye, and drill them out with the ⅛-inch diameter drill. Next, fit the arms together so that you have a matching pair—with the palms facing towards the body—slide brass washers between rubbing surfaces, and tap the wooden pivots in place;

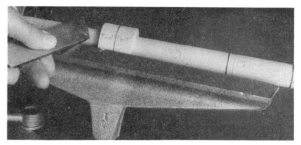

5–12   Use the heel of the skew chisel to skim the surface to a super-smooth finish.

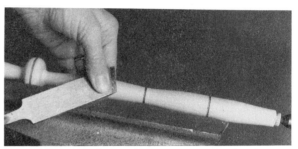

5–13   Support the workpiece—to stop it bending—while at the same time using your thumb to bring the tool into contact with the wood.

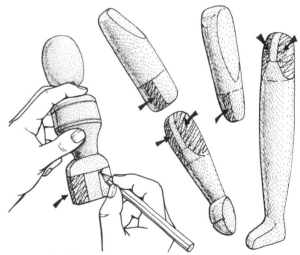

5–14   Shade in all the joint areas that need to be cut away—elbows, knees, and hips.

leave plenty of length so that the pivots can be removed (see 5–15, top). When you come to screwing the arms and legs in place, aim for an easy but firm fit.

Lastly, cut a little mortise hole for the nose (see 5–15, bottom), whittle a scrap of wood to a nose shape and glue it in place.

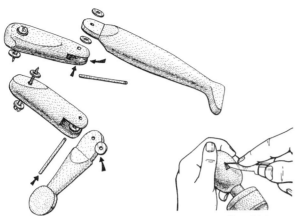

5–15 (Top) Set brass washers between all rubbing surfaces. (Bottom) Use a penknife to cut the mortise hole for the nose—use a series of angled slicing cuts.

PAINTING

Take out all of the screws and pegs, wipe away the dust, and move to the clean area that you have set aside for painting. Start by giving all the parts a thin "sealer" coat of varnish, and hang them on a wire line to dry. When they are completely dry, give them a swift rubdown with fine-grade sandpaper, and wipe them with a damp cloth to remove dust.

Study the painting grid (see 5–16). Paint the head, neck and upper chest, lower arms, and hands a beige pink color. Next, paint in the white socks, the white blouse, the blue bodice, the black hair, the black shoes, and so on. Lay the paint on as simple flat areas of color.

Once the paint is completely dry, give all the components a couple of coats of clear varnish.

Finally, put the doll back together, glue the pegs in place, sand down the ends of the pegs, and make good any damaged areas with paint and varnish. The doll is finished and ready to be dressed.

TROUBLESHOOTING AND POSSIBLE MODIFICATIONS

• If you are working on a very small lathe, then it's a good idea to clear away some of the waste before mounting the workpiece. All you do is establish the end centers by drawing crossed diagonals, scribe circles out on the

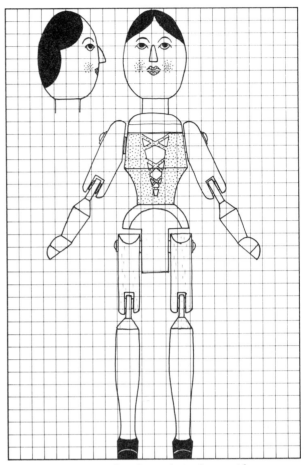

5–16 Painting grid—the scale is three grid squares to one inch. Note the "laced" design on the bodice/blouse.

ends of the wood, draw tangents at the circle-diagonal crossover points, draw lines from the resultant octagons to establish the along-the-wood waste, and then clear the waste with a rasp or plane.

• If you are at all worried about fitting the joints, then it's a good idea to have a try-out on a piece of scrap wood. You could, for instance, cut a practice joint on the end of a piece of dowel.

• If you like the idea of the doll, but have in mind to go for a quicker and stronger option—say as a present for a particular child—then you could leave out the joints at the elbows and knees.

• 6 •

Set of Clown Skittles and Two Balls

A set of nine identical skittles—all painted with clown imagery—plus two balls

In the United States, Europe, and Britain, the game of skittles, skittle pins, or ninepins has long been associated with those who have lots of fun without too much thought to the future—this is sometimes described as "all beer and skittles."

It's interesting to note that, although the game of skittles has been around for a very long time—with just about everyone from the ancient Greeks, Romans, and Egyptians, as well as Scots, Irish, Germans, Dutch and French playing—it has always been played with nine skittles or pins (see 6–1).

So why, in the United States, does one play with ten pins? Well, at the beginning of the twentieth century, a law was passed in the United States specifically banning

the game of ninepins—because its popularity was allegedly affecting the economic output of the country. The players, not to be beaten, added another skittle or pin, called the game "Tenpins," and carried on playing!

From a woodturning viewpoint, the attraction of making a set of skittles lies in the challenge of making the balls and the repeat shapes; it is a skill-expanding undertaking. If you can turn out a set of nine nearly identical skittles, and make a couple of matched balls, then you can turn just about anything!

If you want to make a game for older children, or even for adults, and if you are looking for a real challenge—perhaps one of the most difficult of all woodturning tasks—then this is the project for you.

6–1 *Project picture.*

DESIGN AND TECHNIQUE BASICS

Before you put tool to wood, make a visit to a folk museum, and get to see how traditional skittles tend to be more or less figure shaped. That is, even when they are unpainted, they usually have a foot, a trunk, a waist, a belly, a chest, a neck, and a head. Make sketches and notes, and generally familiarize yourself with skittle shapes, sizes, and types.

Although we describe the project as difficult, this is not to say that making one ball and one skittle is a problem—although turning a ball is always a little bit tricky. The real difficulty is making repeats or multiples of any turning. It requires a lot of patience and an eye for detail.

Woodturning Tip

Bearing in mind that "identical" is a relative term—after all, even four, turned table legs are never really identical—it's a good idea to make more turnings than you need. For example, you might make, twelve skittles, and then choose the best nine.

Have a look at the turning stages (see 6–2, top and middle), and see how, from skittle to skittle, the profile is read off and checked with a cardboard template. That is, once the primary lines have been set in, and the turning is well under way, the template is used to confirm and fine check that all is well.

Consider how, although all nine skittles have the same clown imagery, they are grouped by color in three sets of three. Finally, note the way that the two balls are turned all-of-a-piece from a single length of wood, while the skittles are turned one at a time.

Lathe and Tool Considerations

Although I favor using a four-jaw chuck for most wood-turning procedures, this is not to say that you can't work this project between centers, use a "special" chuck, or even make a wooden chuck specifically to turn these

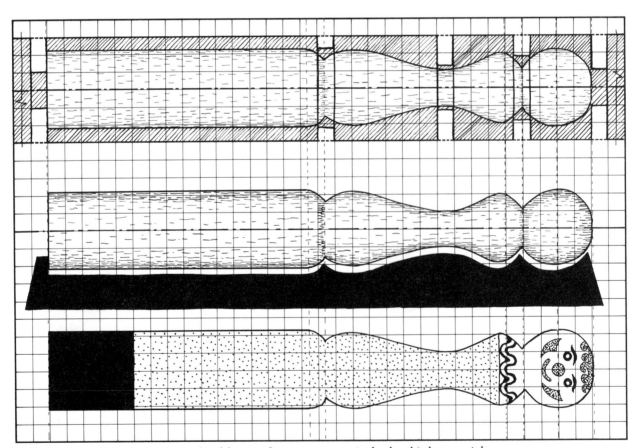

6–2 *Working drawings—at a scale of four grid squares to one inch, the skittles are eight inches high, and a little over one inch in diameter. Note the cardboard template.*

skittles. This is one of those beautifully flexible projects that lets you go your own way. That said, if the wood is well supported in a chuck, then you can easily move the tailstock center out of the way, and bring the head of the skittle to a super-smooth finish before parting off. Certainly special chucks are expensive items, but, then again, they are great time-savers.

Tools and Equipment

Apart from a lathe, you need—
• square gouge
• round-nosed gouge
• parting tool
• skew chisel
• both dividers and callipers
• pencil and ruler
• sheet each of tracing and workout paper
• length of stiff card (cardboard)
• pair of scissors
• pack of graded sandpapers
• paintbrushes—a broad and a fine point
• selection of acrylic paints in the colors black, white, red, yellow, and blue
• small can of high-gloss varnish

Wood

For this project you need a 12-inch length of hard, dense-grained wood 1½ by 1½ inch square for each skittle that you want to make. We've selected beech, but you could use straight-grained pine, lime/basswood, or just about any straight-grained, knot-free wood that comes to hand.

You also need, a seven-inch length of hard, dense-grained wood 2½ by 2½ inches square for the two balls. The seven-inch length allows for a good amount of waste.

Toymaking Tip

If you like the idea of turning the skittles, but aren't so keen on making the balls, then there's no reason why you can't buy a couple of dense rubber balls.

TOYMAKING STAGES

Making the Skittles—Mounting the Wood on the Lathe and Setting Out

Once you have your tools in order, have checked the wood over, and generally have made ready for the task ahead, draw a skittle out to full size, and make a clear

tracing. Draw in a clear center line that runs from the base through to the head. To make a template press-transfer the half-skittle image onto the stiff card, modify the ends to accommodate the waste wood at the either end of the skittle (see 6–2, middle), and cut it out with scissors.

Being aware that all nine skittles are to be identical, take one of your 12-inch lengths of wood, give it a swift check over to make sure that it's free from nasties, establish the end center points by drawing crossed diagonals, and mount the wood securely on the lathe. Bring the T-rest up to the work, turn the wood over by hand to make sure that it spins freely, run through your checklist, and switch on the power.

Woodturning Safety Tip

For safety's sake, always make sure that the tool rest—usually called either rest or T-rest—is well positioned before switching on the power. Be warned, if the wood is other than square in cross section and you set the rest hard up against the short side, then the workpiece is likely to strike the tool rest twice in a full revolution. This being so, always turn the wood by hand through a couple of full revolutions—just to be sure—before the power is switched on.

When you are ready to go, take the gouge—the one with the square cut end—and swiftly turn the wood down to the largest possible round section. This done, change over to using the large skew chisel, and spend time fine-tuning your skills by turning the wood down to a good, smooth finish. And so you continue, repeatedly skimming down with the skew chisel and checking with the calliper, until you have a beautifully smooth cylinder at 1½ inches in diameter.

Setting Out the Step-Offs and Sinking the Waste

When you have achieved a crisp 1½ inch diameter cylinder—the smoother the better—then take the dividers, and carefully transfer the primary measurements from the tracing to the workpiece. With the head of the skittle at the tailstock end, and working from right to left along the wood, allow a small amount for tailstock waste, and then step off one inch for the head, ¼ inch for the top of the ruff, about 2¾ inches for the top of body, ¼ inch for the hips, and lastly 3⅞ inches for the base—that is, from the waist down to the base line. Have a look at the working drawings, and see how each of the step-offs is marked with a dotted line (see 6–2, top). While you are running your eyes over the working drawing, note how the profile relates closely to the primary cylinder in that the high points are more or less the full diameter, and the low points—the V-cuts—tend not to dip by much more than 1/4 inch.

With the step-off marks in place, take the parting tool and sink the "sizing" or pilot cuts to the required depth. Use the callipers for accurate sizing (see 6–3). Center and sink one cut on the neck line, one at the narrowest point between the neck and the waist, and one at the waist. Sink the waste at the head and the base. Don't cut too deeply, just enough to clear the bulk of the waste and establish the "core" diameter. If you cut too deeply into the waist you will end up with an unwanted stepped effect. Clearly pencil-label areas, and check all of the measurements before you continue (see 6–4).

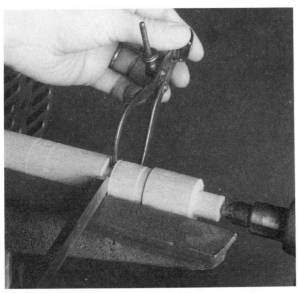

6–3 Use the callipers to achieve accurate sizing.

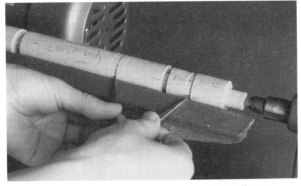

6–4 Make several checks to ensure that all is correct—if it helps, pencil label the various parts.

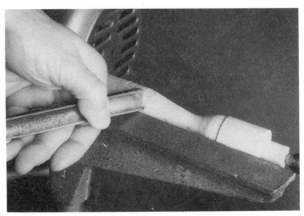

6–5 Lay the side of the gouge against the high spot, and cut a shallow groove.

Turning the Skittle Profile

Having established the length of the skittle, and the position of the dips—by sinking five carefully placed "sizing" cuts—take the skew chisel and start to turn and define the "valleys." Take the gouge of your choice, and turn down the long, slow, easy urn-shaped tapered curve that goes to make the profile between the waist and the ruff. Start by laying the side of the gouge on the high spot; engage the edge to make a shallow groove (see 6–5), and then roll the blade in a long, slow, easy scooping motion to clear the waste and cut the curve. Run repeatedly down from the ruff into the dip, and then down from the waist into the dip (see 6–6), until you achieve the correct profile. Tidy up the bottom of the dip to complete the form.

For cutting the waist, the procedure is to use the toe of the skew chisel to deepen the valley (see 6–7), and then turn the chisel over, and use the heel to round-over the curves at each side of the valley (see 6–8). Don't try to complete a curve with a single cut, but rather, make a series of passes until the desired profile has been achieved. If you are working as described, the blade should finish up in the vertical position, with the heel in the valley and the toe uppermost. Use the same method to turn the shape of the head (see 6–9).

Proceed, adjusting a V-cut with the toe of the skew chisel, checking with the callipers, adjusting the curves with the gouge, checking with the template, and so on, until, little-by-little, you achieve all the curves that make up the design. The secret is to keep your tools sharp, to take your time, and to be careful that you don't snag and catch the wood with the wrong part of the bevel.

When you have what you consider is a well turned skittle, and when it nicely fits the template, use the toe of

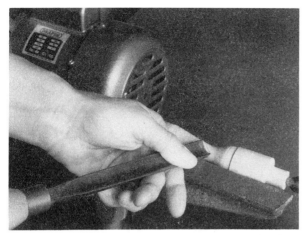

6–6   *As you advance, roll the gouge over to finish up at the lowest part of the valley with the tool sitting upright.*

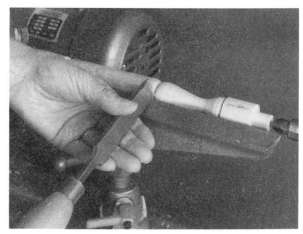

6–7   *Use the long point—the "toe"—of the skew chisel to deepen the valley.*

the skew chisel to part off the head from the waste. Wind the tailstock back out of the way, give the skittle and the whole works a quick rub down with fine-grade sandpaper, and part off. Continue, repeating the procedure, again and again, until you have a full set of skittles.

Woodturning Tip

When you are turning a tall, slender form that needs to sit/stand fair and square on a level surface—like a skittle—make sure, when you are parting off, that you slightly undercut or "dish" the base. That is, make sure that the base is concave.

6–8   *Travel from high to low wood, all the while using the heel to turn the round shoulder profile.*

6–9   *At one and the same time, raise the tool handle so that the heel bites, cuts, and shapes the ball-like head.*

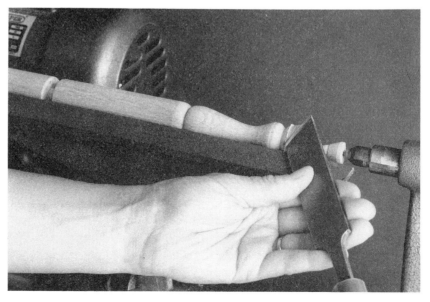

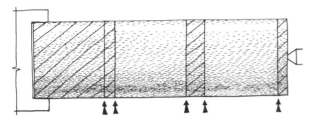

6–10 *Set out the step-offs that go to make up the two balls—¼ inch for tailstock waste, two inches for the first ball, ½ inch for between-ball waste, two inches for the second ball, and the remainder for waste.*

6–11 *Advance the parting tool to sink the waste to a depth of about 1¼ inches.*

6–12 *Use the toe of the skew chisel to cut a very shallow V-cut at the halfway high spot—on both balls.*

Turning the Two Balls

Take the seven-inch length of 2½ by 2½ inch square section of wood—the piece for the two balls—check it over for possible problems, and mount it on the lathe, as already described. Start by turning the wood down to a smooth two-inch diameter cylinder. Once again, swiftly clear the bulk of the waste with the large square-ended gouge, and then use the skew to tidy up the finish.

Take the divider and set out the step-offs from the tailstock end in the sequence ¼ inch for tailstock waste, two inches for the first ball, ½ inch for between-ball parting waste, two inches for the second ball, ½ inch for parting waste, and the remainder for chuck waste (see 6–10). Divide each ball in half with a one-inch shallow-cut step-off—just to mark out the halfway point, or you might say the greatest diameter.

When you are content with the arrangement, take the parting tool and sink the three bands of waste to a depth of 1¼ inches—so that you are left with a central core of about ½ inch (see 6–11). Take the skew, and use the toe to set the high spots of the two balls in with a very shallow V-cut (see 6–12). Starting with the half-ball nearest the tailstock, rest the chisel flat-down on the high spot—so that the blade is "looking" towards the tailstock—raise the handle until the heel of the bevel begins to bite, and then advance and roll the chisel in one continuous movement to turn the shape of the first half-ball. And so continue to take cuts—bite-advance-and-roll, bite-advance-and-roll (see 6–13), all the while, cutting off the shoulder of waste, and gradually bringing the half-ball to shape. With the first half-ball neatly turned to shape, all you do is turn the chisel over so that the blade is "looking" in the other direction, and repeat the procedure for the other side.

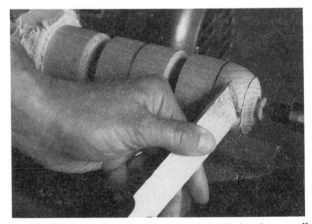

6–13 *Repeatedly bite-advance and roll the skew—all the while working from high to low wood.*

Clockwise from upper left: Czechoslovakian trumpet or horn in the shape of a lady's head (Project 12); Jumping Jack figure with string-operated fly-up arms and legs (Project 3); Pull-string spinning top (Project 9).

A

Farm tractor and trailer (Project 15). The tractor has steerable front wheels, swivel bucket seat, headlights, and hitching peg. Trailer has steerable front wheels and a load of logs.

Nutcracker in the shape of a nineteenth century German soldier (Project 10).

C

Pull-along toy with two tumbler acrobats (Project 13).

Clockwise from upper left: Stand-up tumble doll (Project 8); Simple turned skittle "baby" doll (Project 1); Cup-and-ball "bilboquet" game (Project 7).

Left: Dutch doll with jointed limbs (Project 5). Right: Rocking horse and rider (Project 14).

Clockwise from upper left: Hollow-turned "lady doll" shaker rattle (Project 2); Round-about, turntable, or merry-go-round with six figures and checkered table cloth (Project 11); Baby's rattle with "captive" rings turned from a single length of wood (Project 4).

G

Set of nine identical skittles, painted with clown imagery, and two balls (Project 6).

6–14   *Cup the ball in one hand and gently part-off.*

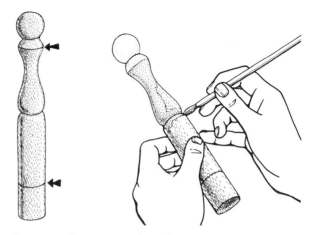

6–15   *(Left) Draw in the color-change guidelines at the ruff and the base. (Right) Start by blocking in the main areas of ground color.*

With the first ball in line finished, move the tailstock back out of the way, use the sandpaper to rub it down to a smooth finish, and part off. The parting off procedure is beautifully simple; all you do is support the ball in one hand—not too tight—advance the parting tool, and gently cut through the remaining stalk of waste (see 6–14). Finally, you reposition the tailstock, and turn the second ball as already described.

FINISHING AND PAINTING

With the turning finished, clear up the debris, wipe the turnings with a slightly damp cloth, and move to the dust-free area that you have set aside for painting. Before you do anything else, have a look at the painting grid (see 6–2, bottom). Notice how, although all the skittles are given the same clown imagery—white faces, black bases, and the same red and black details—the skittles are grouped in three teams by painting the main part of the body in the team color. We have gone for the team colors red, yellow, and blue.

Having studied the color grid, and drawn in the color-change guidelines at the base and the ruff (see 6–15, left), take the large paintbrush and the well-mixed acrylic colors, and lay on the main areas of ground color (see 6–15, bottom)—white from the top of the head to the underside of the ruff, red, yellow or blue for the ruff to the base line, and black for the base. As needed, and not forgetting to lightly sand between coats, lay on a second coat for good coverage.

When the ground colors are dry, first use a pencil to draw in the features, (see 6–2, bottom), and then paint them in with the fine-point paintbrush—red for the hair, nose, mouth, and cheeks, and black for the eyes, brows, and ruff. Paint each ball, one half red and the other half blue. It is best to paint them one half at a time and to let them dry between halves.

Finally, when the colors are completely dry, lay on a couple of coats of clear varnish. Wow! Zapp! Cat-Chunk!—the skittles are ready for fun!

TROUBLESHOOTING AND POSSIBLE MODIFICATIONS

- If you are working on a large lathe with a hefty chuck, then you could perhaps turn four skittles all-of-a-piece from a single length of wood. If you do go for this option, turn them in pairs head to head.
- If you are at all worried about the project—say making the balls—then it's a good idea to have a try-out on a piece of scrap wood.
- If you like the idea of skittles, but you are not so keen on the thought of your children throwing wooden balls around the house, then consider substituting soft foam balls.
- If you do work between centers, allow for slightly more waste at the tailstock.

·7·

Bilboquet Game

A cup and ball game—the captive ball is flicked up into the air and caught in the cup—a game of skill

Bilboquet, or you might know it as Cup and Ball or Ball in a Cup, is one of those timeless traditional games that can be found all over the world (see 7–1). I've seen a leather and bone bilboquet that was made in the nineteenth century by American Indians, a wood and ivory version that was made in England in the sixteenth century, a curious twig and seed pod type that was made in Hawaii in the late nineteenth century, and I could continue listing all manner of bilboquets that were made variously in Mexico, France, India, Japan, China, and just about every country that you can think of. Captain Cook, for instance, saw the game being played by both the South Sea islanders, and by "Indians" on the American Northwest Coast.

Although from country to country there are many material and constructional variations—paper cones, balls stuffed with feathers and hair, pointed sticks instead of cups, and shuttlecocks instead of balls—the basic theme is much the same. A ball or shuttlecock is flicked up into the air and caught in a cup or cone—like a ball being caught in a pair of cupped hands.

If you want to make a game with a pedigree, one that was played by just about everyone from Captain Cook to Pocahontas, then this is the project for you.

DESIGN AND TECHNIQUE BASICS

Before you rush to your lathe, visit the nearest museum, and see just how many variations there are on the cup-and-ball theme. In the light of your own research, you might well decide to modify our project.

Have a look at the project picture (see 7–1) and the working drawings (see 7–2). Consider how the game is made from two components—a slender hand-held cup, and a ball. The cup is slightly unusual in that it can be stood on its base and displayed, like a trophy or an egg in a cup. Look at the cross section on the working drawing, and see the way we have simplified the hollowing out stage by using a large diameter drill bit to bore out the bulk of the waste. Certainly if you did all the hollowing out on the lathe, you might well achieve a smoother cup form, but that's for you to decide.

If you like the idea of making the cup, but are not so keen on turning the ball, then there's nothing to stop you from using a shop-bought ball. Or then again, you could perhaps go for an upmarket version, and make the cup and ball from precious, exotic woods such as box or rosewood. It needs thinking about!

Lathe and Tool Considerations

Bearing in mind that with both the cup and the ball, the turning stages are that much easier if the tailstock can be wound back out of the way, this is one of those projects that is best worked with a chuck. We chose to use a four-jaw chuck.

7–1   Project picture.

For ease of working, we chose to clear the bulk of the inside-cup waste with a 1½-inch diameter Forstner bit. If you don't have such a bit, then you could clear the waste with a round-nosed scraper.

Tools and Equipment

Apart from a lathe, you need—
- square gouge
- round-nosed gouge
- parting tool
- skew chisel
- round-nosed scraper
- bench drill press with a 1½-inch Forstner bit
- both dividers and callipers
- pencil and ruler
- sheet each of tracing and workout paper
- piece of stiff card (cardboard) for the ball template
- pair of scissors
- pack of graded sandpapers
- paintbrushes—a broad and a fine point

- acrylic paints in the colors blue and green
- small can of high-gloss varnish

Wood

For this project you need two lengths of easy-to-turn wood three by three inches square—a 12-inch length for the cup, and a piece about five inches long for the ball. We've chosen to use jelutong, but you could just as well select boxwood, cherry, plum, lime, or whatever—as long as it's smooth grained and free from knots. Note that you could, in fact, turn both items from a single length of wood.

TOYMAKING STAGES

Making the Cup—Mounting the Wood on the Lathe and Setting Out

Once you have studied the working drawings (see 7–2), gathered together all your tools and materials, drawn the

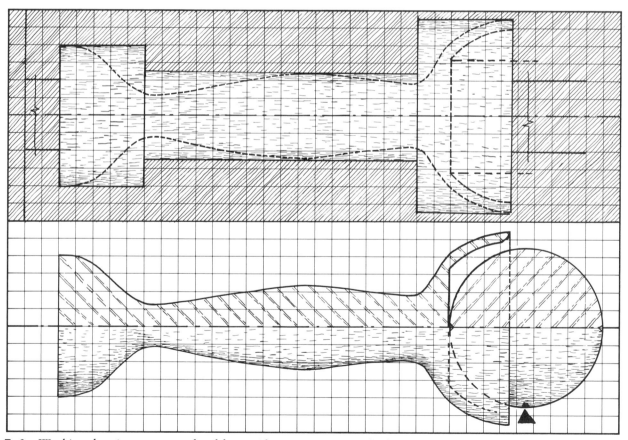

7–2 Working drawings—at a scale of four grid squares to one inch, the total ball-in-a-cup game stands about eight inches high and is 2¾ inches wide across the diameter of the cup.

design up to full size, and made a clear tracing, give the 12-inch length of wood a last check over—just to make sure that it's free from knots and splits—and mount it securely on the lathe. This done, take the gouge and the skew chisel, and turn the wood down to a smooth cylinder that is a little under three inches in diameter.

Take the divider and, working from left to right along the wood, set in all the step-offs that go to make the design. Allow a generous amount for chuck waste and then 1¼ inches for the base, four inches for the slender handle, 1⅜ inches for the cup, and the remainder for tailstock waste. With the guide marks in place, take the calliper and the parting tool, and run two guide cuts into each of the three step-offs. Aim for core diameters of two inches for the base, 1¼ inches for the handle, and 2¾ inches for the cup. Refer to the working drawing (see 7–2, top).

Sinking the Waste and Turning the Outside Profile

With the pilot cuts in place—two in each step-off—take the gouge, and start by clearing the bulk of the waste from the handle area. Cut down to within a whisker of the 1¼ inch core diameter. Repeat the procedure with the base and the cup. Having removed the bulk of the waste with the gouge, take the skew chisel, and clean up the three steps so that you have, as it were, a form that is made up from three cleanly stepped cylinders—a bit like a dumbbell (see 7–3).

Woodturning Tip

Although it isn't strictly necessary to use the skew chisel to clean up the steps at all the stages along the way, we find that it helps to bring the workpiece to order at each stage. Meaning that the clean cut surfaces enable us to see what's going on—the run of the grain, the true diameters at primary points, the character of the wood, how much wood we can play around with, and so on.

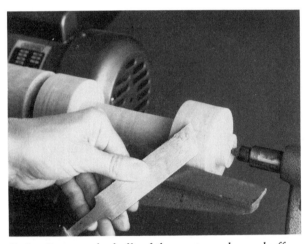

7–3   Remove the bulk of the waste, and round off the sharp corners so that you have a smooth-curved dumb-bell shape.

Take the square-end gouge, and, working from high to low wood—that is, from each end down towards the handle—swiftly turn the angled steps so that you have a smooth profile. The working procedure is to set the gouge side-down on the high spot so that the inside is "looking" in the direction of the cut, and to run the gouge in a slow rolling action down the curve and into the valley (see 7–4). The actual shape of the handle, base, and cup aren't too important as long as the curves flow smoothly one into another, the handle is comfortable to hold, and the cup is large enough to hold the ball.

When you have achieved what you consider is a comfortable, pleasing-to-the-eye shape, take the skew chisel and skim the wood down to a good finish. Being careful not to catch the toe of the chisel on the top of the base or the underside of the cup, set the bevel flat-down on the high spots, face the heel in the direction of the cut, lift the handle slightly until the blade begins to bite, and then advance in the direction of the cut. Many beginners are a bit worried about using the skew chisel. But don't worry; the secret is to use a razor sharp tool, to work with a light touch, and to keep the blade at as flat an angle as possible. Continue skimming off the wood—little by little—until you have a smooth, curved form. Finally, rub the whole workpiece down with fine-grade sandpaper.

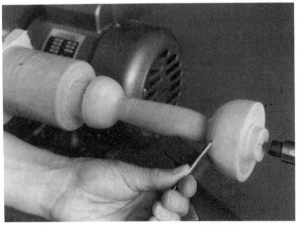

7–4   Run the gouge down in a smooth rolling movement—down the curve and into the valley.

7–5 *Use the toe of the chisel to make a V-cut to the waste side of the rim. Cut a deep furrow between the rim and the center of waste.*

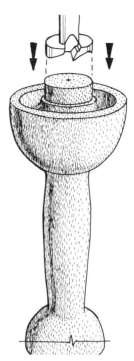

7–6 *Run the Forstner bit down into the cup to re-move the bulk of the waste. Make repeated checks with the calliper to ensure that there is enough wall thickness.*

Hollowing Out the Cup

With the workpiece still being pivoted between the chuck and the tailstock center, swing the tool rest around so that you can approach the cup end-on; then take the skew chisel and mark out the thickness of the cup rim. Use the toe of the chisel to make a V-cut to the waste side of the rim. Aim for a rim thickness about ³⁄₁₆-inch thick (see 7–5). Cut as deeply as you can; concentrate on shaping the inside-cup wall. When the cone of waste at the middle of the cup starts to get in the way, turn off the power, give the chuck a few turns with the key—just to make sure that the wood is firmly secured in the jaws—then, draw the tailstock out of the way. Remove the whole works from the lathe, with the wood still in the chuck, and move to the bench drill press. With a 1½-inch Forstner bit in the drill, and with the workpiece gripped in the chuck, position the bit on the dimple left by the tailstock center, and run the bit into the cup to a depth of about ⅞ inch (see 7–6). If you look at the working drawings, you will see that the depth of the hole will depend very much on the outside shape or profile of the cup. The easiest way of working is to run the drill bit repeatedly in and out of the wood, all the while checking with the calliper as to the thickness of wood at the bottom of the cup.

Woodturning Tip

If you look at the working drawings, you will see that we could have easily deepened the cup by first using the large bit—as described—and then following with a one-inch bit, and drilling the hole ¼-inch deeper.

When you have drilled the hole as deep as you dare, pencil-mark the center point, remount the whole works back on the lathe, wind the tailstock center back in so that it pivots on the inside-cup center, and then switch on the power. If you are lucky, the wood will still be well centered and true!

If all is well and as described, wind the tailstock center back out of the way, and reposition the tool rest so that you can work the wood end-on. Use the round-nosed scraper very cautiously to hollow out the inside walls down to the level of the bottom of the bored-out hole, and to generally make the cup smooth. Finally, rub the whole workpiece down with fine-grade sandpaper and part-off from the lathe.

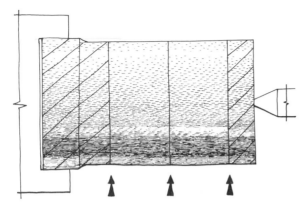

7–7 Take the dividers and, working from the tail-stock end, set out the step-offs in the sequence ½ inch for the tailstock waste, 1⅛ inch for the first half-ball, 1⅛ inch for the second half-ball, and the remainder for waste.

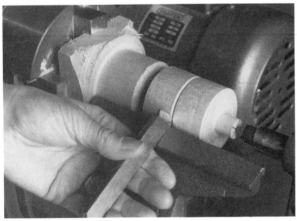

7–8 Use the toe of the skew to set in the high spot of the ball with a shallow V-cut.

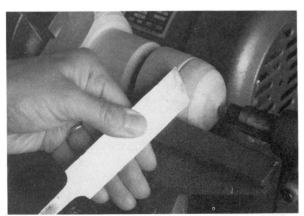

7–9 Take repeated cuts until you have a good half-ball shape.

Turning the Ball

Start by drawing a 2¼-inch-diameter circle on the cardboard and making yourself a template. All you need is a quarter-circle profile that you can use to check the shape of the ball (look ahead to 7–10).

When you have made the template, take the other length of wood—the piece for the ball—check it over for possible problems, and mount it on the lathe, as already described. Start by turning the wood down to a smooth, 2¼-inch diameter cylinder. Once again, swiftly clear the bulk of the waste with the gouge, and then use the skew chisel to tidy up.

Take the divider and, working from the tailstock end, set out the step-offs in the sequence ½ inch for tailstock waste, 1⅛ inches for the first half-ball, 1⅛ inches for the second half-ball, and the remainder for waste (see 7–7). Don't cut the halfway mark too deep, just enough to mark out the greatest diameter. When you are happy that all is correct, take the parting tool and sink the waste at either end of the ball so that you are left with a central core of waste about ½ inch in diameter.

Take the skew, and use the toe to set the high spot of the ball in with a shallow V-cut (see 7–8). Now, starting with the half-ball nearest the tailstock, rest the chisel flat-down on the high spot—so that the blade is "looking" towards the tailstock—raise the handle until the heel of the bevel begins to bite, and then advance-and-roll the chisel in one continuous movement to turn down the shape of the first half-ball.

Woodturning Tip

Only take thin shavings, all the while stopping to assess your progress. You could even pencil-in areas that need to be worked. Try to avoid the classic mistake of having a flat area on either side of the midline.

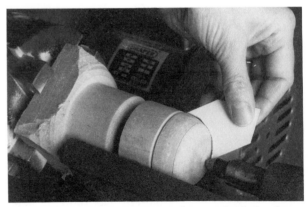

7–10 Use the cardboard template to check the shape.

Continue making cuts; bite-advance-and-roll, bite-advance-and-roll, all the while, cutting off the shoulder of waste and getting nearer to the half-ball to shape (see 7–9). Use the template to check your progress (see 7–10).

With the first half of the ball neatly turned to shape, flip the chisel over so that the blade is "looking" in the other direction, and repeat the procedure for the other half of the ball.

When you have a cleanly turned, well-balanced ball—and that isn't easy!—move the tailstock back out of the way, use the sandpaper to rub it down to a smooth finish, and part-off. The parting-off procedure is to support the ball in one hand—not too tightly—advance the parting tool, and gently cut through the remaining stalk of waste.

Finally, drill a hole into one side of the ball for the string (refer to 7–2).

FINISHING AND PAINTING

As always, when the turnings are finished, clean up the debris, wipe the turnings with a slightly damp cloth, and move to the dust-free area that you have set aside for painting.

Study the painting grid (see 7–11), and draw the color-change guidelines on the cup and the ball. Take the large paintbrush, and give the whole works a thin sealer coat of varnish. When the varnish is dry, use the fine-grade sandpaper to rubdown the nibs. This done, take a clean paintbrush and the well-mixed acrylic colors, and lay on the areas of color—green for one half of the ball, green for the base and cup, and blue for the other half of the ball and for the slender part of the cup handle. As needed, apply another coat for coverage, sanding between coats.

Painting/Varnishing Tip

It's a good idea to set the ball in an eggcup, and paint/varnish one half of the ball at a time.

When the colors are dry, lay on a couple of coats of clear varnish, fix the string in place—pegged in the ball hole and tied around the cup handle. You are ready for fun! Stand back! Careful of hitting yourself in the head or hands . . . it's amazing!

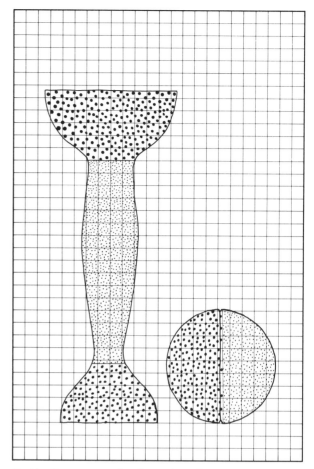

7–11   Painting grid—the scale is four grid squares to one inch. Note that the inside of the cup is painted blue.

TROUBLESHOOTING AND POSSIBLE MODIFICATIONS

- If you like the idea of the game, but are worried about the weight of the ball, then consider using a soft foam ball.
- To give the imagery a bit of pizazz, you could apply small stick-on colored shapes before varnishing.
- What about going for a really tricky game/project, and have a cup on either end of the handle?
- If you have a tailstock chuck, then you could bore out the hole while the workpiece is still on the lathe.

· 8 ·

Stand-Up Tumble Doll

A small tumble doll—if you give her a little push, she wobbles over and stands up again

Not so many years ago, just about every child had a tumbler doll (see 8–1). Known variously in the United States and Britain as wibble-wobbles, wibblies, tumblers, Kelly's, tilters, and Fanny Royd's—in France as poupee boule—in Japan as Ot-tok-l—and in Germany as Putzelmann—these beautiful, easy-to-make traditional toys must surely rate as one of the most amusing and popular playthings of all time.

They are great fun; give them a push, and they fall over, do a little wibble-wobble dance, and stand right up again. I've seen them made from wood, papier-mâché, pressed tinplate, gourds, plastic, and just about every material that you care to think of.

It's easy to see why these toys have remained so popular; who could not find pleasure in a little doll that always comes back for more? How and why do they stand up? Kids are fascinated by the mystery. From the woodturning/toymaking viewpoint, they are beautifully direct. No batteries, springs, strings or fancy motors; no more or less than a lead weight that is concealed deep in the half-ball base.

If you enjoy making small tricky turnings, and if you have a liking for small enigmatic toys, then you are going to love this project.

THOUGHTS ON DESIGN AND TECHNIQUE

When you have studied traditional stand-up dolls in general, and this doll in particular (refer to 8–1), have a good, long look at the working drawings (see 8–2). Note how the turnings are made all-of-a-piece, with the ball-base being drilled, and the top of the doll being used to plug the weight hole.

The tricky part of this project is turning the lady's "waist"—the plug—down to a slight taper so that it is a good tight push-fit in the weight hole. Certainly it looks easy—but it isn't! If the fit is too tight, there is a danger that the ball will split, and if it's too loose, then the top of the lady slides into the hole.

Woodturning Wisdom

My grandad used to say, "*Almost* all right . . . is completely all wrong!"

Be aware that the height of the figure and the position of the weight in the hole are both critical factors. If the total height is greater than 5½ inches and/or the lead weight is not far enough down in the hole, then the tumble doll stays tumbled down when she's pushed over. If you do decide to make modifications, be mindful of the relationship between height and weight. If you want to go for a bigger doll, then be ready to deepen and broaden the hole—and add extra weight.

8–1 Project picture.

Lathe and Tool Considerations

As with all of these projects, we use a four-jaw chuck to hold the wood secure. You could just as well use a wooden chuck and/or you could change the working order somewhat and turn between centers. But we always feel that using the chuck is the easiest and safest way of getting the job done.

The other main consideration, is how to accurately drill the weight hole. We solved the problem, by taking the whole works off the lathe—the chuck complete with the ball—boring the hole out on the bench drill press, and then going back to the lathe.

Woodturning Tip

If you have a tailstock drill chuck, so much the better; all you do is bore out the hole while the workpiece is on the lathe.

Tools and Equipment

Apart from a lathe, you need—
- gouge
- parting tool
- skew chisel
- bench drill press
- 1½ inch diameter Forstner drill bit
- both dividers and callipers
- pencil and ruler
- sheet each of tracing and workout paper
- pack of graded sandpapers
- small quantity of plumber's lead
- tin can for melting lead
- Super Glue
- two soft-haired watercolor paintbrushes—a broad and a fine point
- acrylic paints in the colors red, dark blue, black, white, yellow, green, and beige pink
- small quantity of clear, high-gloss varnish

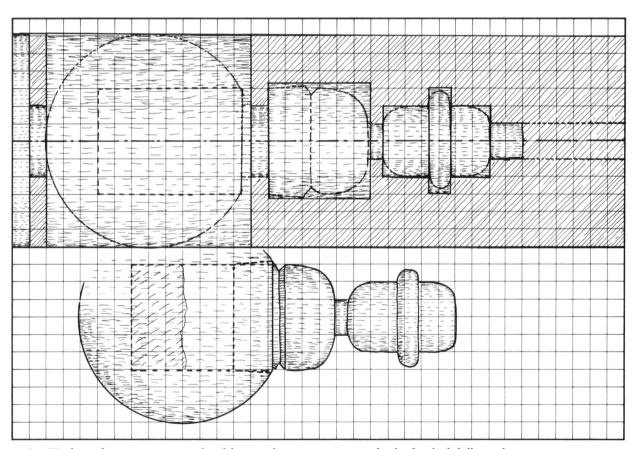

8–2   *Working drawings—at a scale of four grid squares to one inch, the finished doll stands 5½ inches high and is almost three inches across the diameter of the ball. Note the tapered plug and the critical diameter of the bodice.*

73

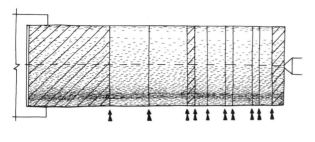

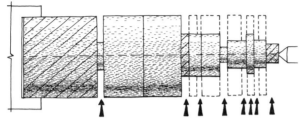

8–3 (Top) Carefully set out all of the step-offs that make up the design. (Bottom) Set out each step-off with a couple of pilot sizing cuts—allow extra waste so that you can cut back to a good finish.

Wood

For this project you need a 10-inch length of easy-to-turn wood three by three inches square.

We have gone for jelutong because it is so lightweight and easy to turn. You may find jelutong to be a bit characterless, but then again, since the whole toy is going to be painted anyway, the color and texture of the grain aren't very important.

TOYMAKING STAGES

Setting Out the Wood and First Cuts

Once you have a clear understanding of how the project needs to be worked and put together, draw the design at full size and make a clear tracing (refer to 8–2). Take your length of wood and check it over to make sure that it's free from flaws.

Woodturning Tip

Checking the wood before turning is always a good idea, but it becomes all the more important when you are drilling large holes.

Establish the end centers by drawing crossed diagonals, mount the wood securely on the lathe, and bring the tool rest up to the work. When you have gone through your pre-switch-on checklist, and generally made sure that you and the lathe are in good safe order, switch on the

power, and swiftly turn the wood down to the largest possible diameter. Although strictly speaking you only need a rough cylinder at this stage, it is always best, especially if you are a beginner, to turn off the bulk of the waste with the large gouge, and then to fine-tune your technique by bringing the wood to a good finish with the skew chisel.

Having turned a clean cylinder, take the ruler and divider, and carefully set out all the step-offs that make up the design (see 8–3, top). Working from right to left—that is, from the tailstock back towards the headstock—allow a small amount for tailstock waste, and then set out the step-offs in the sequence ½ inch for the crown of the hat, ¼ inch for the brim, ¾ inch for the face, ¼ inch for the neck, about ¾ inch for the chest, ½ inch for the taper, ¼ inch for waste, 1½ inches for the top of the ball, and 1½ inches for the base. Cut the step-offs in clearly with the points of the dividers.

Woodturning Tip

The easiest and safest procedure for marking out the step-offs, is to take your accurately sharpened wood-turning dividers, set it to the required measurement, hold it firmly down on the tool rest, and carefully advance the points so that they score grooves on the spinning cylinder.

Turning the Steps and Cutting the Profile Curves

With the step-offs all painstakingly set out and checked, take the callipers and parting tool, and set each step-off out with a couple of pilot or sizing cuts (see 8–3, bottom). Of course, if the step-off is only the width of the parting tool, then all you need do is run the tool in to the desired depth, and the job is done.

See to it, that the depth of the cuts relate to the size of the core diameter. So, for example, if you start out with a three-inch diameter cylinder and you want to turn a step down to a diameter of 1½ inches, then the pilot cut at that point needs to be ¾ inch deep.

Having set out the depth cuts—the procedure is called "sizing"—take the small gouge and the skew chisel, and turn the waste down to the bottom of the depth cuts (see 8–4). From right to left along the work-piece, the crown of the hat measures about one inch in diameter, the brim 1⅜ inch, the face one inch, the neck ½ inch, the bodice 1½ inches, and the ball as near as possible to three inches in diameter.

When you have accomplished all the step-off diameters, take the skew chisel, and—having first used the toe of the skew chisel to set-in the meridian line with a V-cut

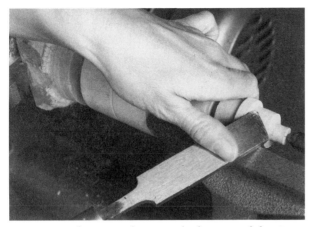

8–4   *Turn the waste down to the bottom of the sizing cuts.*

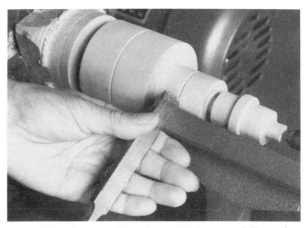

8–5   *Use the toe of the skew chisel to carefully and precisely set-in the meridian lines.*

or groove (see 8–5)—set to work turning down the various curves, beads, and shoulders that make up the design. So, for example, with the large ball turn the chisel over on its side, and use first the heel and then the toe to work downhill on either side of the V-cut. That is, first clear the sharp corner and start the curve with the heel of the chisel (see 8–6), and then, as gradually you get nearer and nearer to the ball shape, turn the tool on its side, and use the side bevel part of the toe to travel around the curve. The trick is to hold the chisel with a nice, easy grip, and to know when to change from heel to toe. As you travel around the side of the ball, keep repositioning the tool rest so that there isn't much of a gap between the blade and the wood.

Woodturning Tip

The wonderful thing about woodturning is that there are many ways of doing the same task. For example, some woodturners—having first used the toe of the skew to mark out the high point—prefer to work the rest of the ball with the heel. It is always best, especially if you have any doubts, to try both methods, and then use the one that works for you.

Continue turning the two halves of the large ball, turning the half-ball bodice (see 8–7), turning the curve of the face, and so on, along the workpiece. Make sure when you are turning the taper—meaning the bit for the plug—that the largest diameter stays at $1\frac{5}{8}$ inches, while the smallest is no smaller than $1\frac{3}{8}$ inches. The idea is that the top of the lady should be a tight push-fit into the base hole so that the bodice groove line comes to rest on, or slightly above, the hole rim.

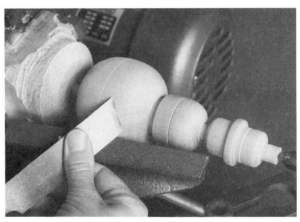

8–6   *Lay the bevel flat-down on the high point, raise the handle until the blade begins to bite, and then run the curve down into the valley.*

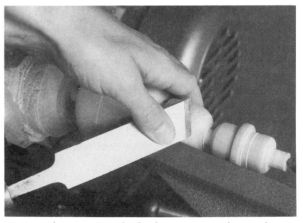

8–7   *When turning the bodice, support the workpiece so that it doesn't become stressed at the thin neck area.*

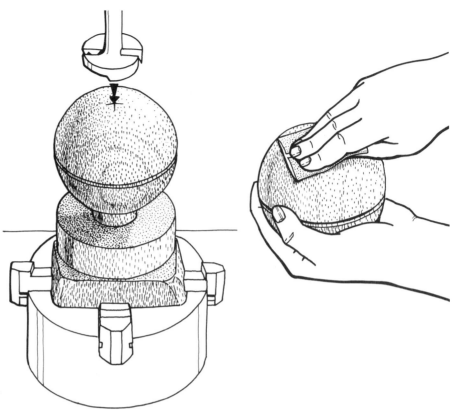

8–8 (Left) Bore the 1½ inch diameter hole about two inches down into the top center of the ball. (Right) Spend time sanding the parting-off point at the bottom of the ball to a smooth, rounded finish.

With all the curves cleanly turned, take a sheet of fine-grade sandpaper, and rub the whole works down to a smooth finish. This done, take the parting tool, and part-off the top of the figure from the lathe and the ball. The order of work is to part-off the small piece of tailstock waste from the hat, draw the tailstock out of the way, support the top of the figure in one hand, and carefully part-off the top of the body from the ball.

Lastly, having repositioned the tool rest so that it is over the bed of the lathe—so that you can work the top of the ball end-on—use the tools of your choice to bring the top of the ball to a good finish.

Boring Out the Ball and Fitting the Lead Weight

With the top of the figure parted off from the ball, and the top of the ball nicely tidied up and marked out with a clear center point, remove the whole works from the lathe—the ball in the chuck—and move to the bench drill press. Arrange the chuck so that the ball is aligned fair and square (see 8–8, left) and run the 1½-inch-diameter hole about two inches down into top center. Test to make sure that the top of the figure has a good push-fit with the hole. As needed, take a slice off the bottom of the tapered plug, and/or sand the rim of the hole, until the bodice line comes to rest just a fraction above the top of the hole.

Return to the lathe and part-off the ball from the waste. As needed, sand the ball to a good finish (see 8–8, right). This done, take the plumber's lead, cut it into small pieces, and fill the ball hole up to a depth of about one inch. Next, melt the lead in an old can, and pour it into the hole.

Heated-Lead Safety Tip

The easiest and safest way to melt the lead is to put it into a clean can, bend the rim into a pouring spout—like a jug—melt the lead over a cooker, and then use a pair of pliers to grip and control the can while you are pouring. Have the ball supported in another can, and make sure that you are working in a totally controlled situation—no kids or pets, plenty of protective clothing, goggles, gloves, and an apron—and maybe a friend to assist.

Wait awhile for the lead to cool, then push the figure into the hole for a try-out. If all is satisfactory, when you push the lady over, she should immediately wobble back into an upright position. If she doesn't, then add a little more lead.

FINISHING AND PAINTING

When you are pleased with the way the tumble doll works, glue the figure in the hole, and move to the dust-free area that you have set aside for painting. Study the painting grid (see 8–9).

If you have used an open-grained wood such as jelutong, start by giving the whole toy a quick coat of varnish to seal the grain. Make sure that the sealing varnish is completely dry, then start by laying on the main areas of color—red for the underside of the ball, blue for the dress, beige pink for the face, and black for the hat. When the ground colors are dry—you may well need to add another coat for good coverage—take the fine-point paintbrush, and pick out all the details that make up the design—the black stripe around the red base, the white apron with the pattern, the red cheeks, nose, and lips, the black eyes, and the red band around the hat.

Lastly, when the acrylic colors are all dry—and after you have, perhaps, signed and dated the base, and/or even given the doll a name—give her a couple of coats of clear varnish, and let the varnish dry. It's time for fun; you will find that you just can't put her down!

TROUBLESHOOTING AND POSSIBLE MODIFICATIONS

- Although this project is pretty straightforward, it's not an easy task to turn a perfect ball or to bore out a weight hole. In fact, the first time around, we drilled the hole so deep that we pushed a hole right through the ball. Don't do as we did—do as we say! It is best not to drill the hole by eye, but rather to work out the precise depth of the hole by drawing the ball at full size and then setting the drill stop at the correct depth.
- If you like the idea of the project, but would prefer to turn the figure all-of-a-piece and not part-off the top of the figure from the ball, you could modify the design, and drill, weight, and plug the bottom of the ball. If you

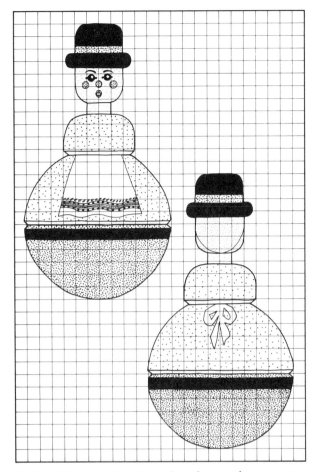

8–9   *Painting grid—the scale is four grid squares to one inch.*

do go for this method, be mindful that the bottom of the ball must be well rounded.
- The ball shape makes the painting a bit tricky. It is best to have the ball supported in a cup or jar, and to paint it in two stages. We painted the top first and then the bottom.

· 9 ·

Pull-String Spinning Top

A spinning top with a built-in pull-string bobbin

Spinning tops—plain and fancy, big and small—must surely rank among the most popular toys of all time! I've seen spinning tops in museums that come from such faraway places in time and space as ancient Greece and Rome, Japan, China, Egypt, Africa, and just about anywhere that you care to imagine. The spinning top is one of those toys that has been around for such a long time, that, really, no one knows when and where it was first invented.

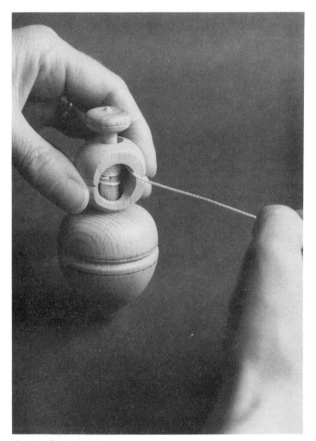

9–1 Project picture.

Some tops need to be whipped, others are spun between the thumb and fingers, and yet others are spun into action by means of a little string-and-crutch launching handle. Our spinning top is extra special in that it has its own built-in pull-string bobbin (see 9–1). It's a beautifully clever idea. In use, the bobbin is held in one hand, the string is swiftly pulled and released with the other, and then the spinning top is calmly set down on a level surface. The great thing is that every shot is a sure-fire success, and, better still, the pull-string self-winds so that the top is always loaded and ready to go.

I've got a feeling that the spinning top was invented by a woodturner! I say this, because not only are the best tops round in section and symmetrical—like everything that comes off the lathe—but, perhaps more to the point, when I look around my workshop, I see that a great many of the little off-cut turnings that litter the floor—little egg and plum shaped pieces of end waste—are by their very nature more or less three-quarters of the way to being spinning tops.

If you are looking for a challenge, and if you know of a fun-loving child who likes playing with complex moving toys, then you are going to enjoy this project!

DESIGN AND TECHNIQUE BASICS

After you have considered all the tool and material implications of making a project of this character, then have a look at the working drawings (see 9–2). Note the way that the three components—the whorl, the bobbin and the spindle—are turned all-of-a-piece from a single length of beech.

The clever thing about this project, is the way that the finished top looks so tidy and pulled-together, almost as if it has evolved, with the making stages all being part and parcel of the natural order of things.

Note the way that the bobbin turning has been drilled in two directions, and then rubbed down in such a way that it becomes more of a ring than a sphere.

If you like the idea of making a top, but want to go for something larger, smaller, or with a different shape, then there's no problem, as long as you bear in mind that the center of gravity needs to be low. That is, if we take it that the total height of the top is about four inches, then it is important that the bulk of the weight be below the two-inch halfway line. I say this, because if your were, for example, to shift the weight by making the top thinner— and maybe having the spindle and bobbin a little bigger—then there is a chance that the top might wobble out of control and flip over. That said, some of the best tops are specifically designed so that they perform by intentionally flipping over.

Finally, consider how the decorative rings have been darkened by friction-burning, and the whole works has been burnished to a high-gloss finish with wax.

Lathe and Tool Considerations

In the context of this project we favor using a four-jaw chuck, for no other reason, than it's such a swift and easy way of pulling a square section of wood to order. Once the wood is secure in the chuck, and the wood is turned down to a round section, then the tailstock can almost be drawn out of the way without worrying about the workpiece spinning off center. This is a great advantage!

As for secondary tooling—meaning tools used off the lathe—the only point to consider is that you do need the use of a ¾-inch diameter Forstner drill bit. You could, no doubt, bore the through-bobbin hole with a twist or flat bit, but, to my mind, such bits are difficult to control, and the resultant holes tend to be rough and ragged.

Woodturning Tip

If you expect to do a lot of woodturning, then really you need to get yourself a set of Forstner drill bits. Drilled holes are an important on-view part of the design; so they need to be smooth faced and flat bottomed. Certainly Forstner drill bits cost more, but then again, they stay sharper longer, they are less likely to break or bend, and the resultant holes are always crisp and clean.

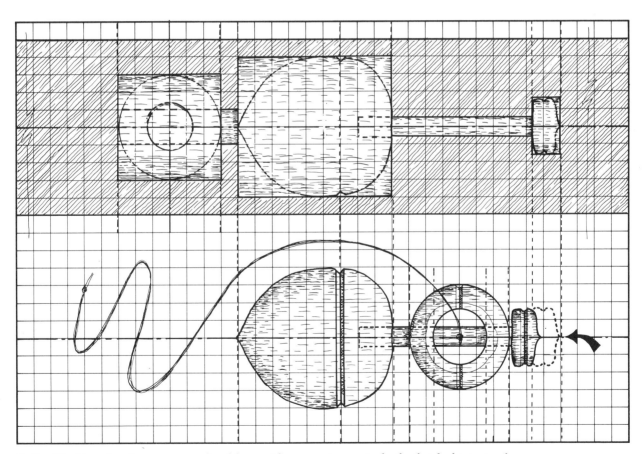

9–2   *Working drawings—at a scale of four grid squares to one inch, the finished top stands about 4¼ inches in height and is two inches in diameter across the widest part of the whorl.*

Tools and Equipment

Apart from a lathe, you need—
- round-nosed gouge
- parting tool
- skew chisel
- both dividers and callipers
- pencil and ruler
- sheet each of tracing and workout paper
- bench drill press
- Forstner drill bits in the sizes—¾ inch, ½ inch, and ⅜ inch—along with a single ¹⁄₁₆-inch twist drill bit
- pack of graded sandpapers
- block or stick of carnauba wax
- pad of cloth for burnishing
- 18-inch length of fine, strong nylon twine—thin enough to pass through a ¹⁄₁₆-inch-diameter hole

Wood

For this project you need a nine-inch length of hard, dense-grained, heavy wood 2¼ by 2¼ inches square—a wood that looks good when waxed. We've gone for beech, but you could just as well select a wood such as box, cherry, or even elm.

Wood Selection Tip

In the context of making traditional woodturned toys, we usually—but not always—go for native European/American pale-colored woods such as beech, lime/linden, pine, elm. We choose these woods, because, on the one hand, they have been tried and tested by generations of toymakers, and, on the other hand, we feel that it's more "green-friendly" to use fast-growing native woods. Such woods are wonderfully easy to use for the simple reason that, since they are pale in color and clean turning—no sticky sap or residue—they are also easy to paint.

TOYMAKING STAGES

Mounting the Wood on the Lathe and First Steps

Once you have considered the project, chosen your wood, made decisions as to your lathe and tools, and generally brought everything to order—tidied up the workshop, told your friends and family what you are working on, and donned your protective gear—then take your length of wood, establish the position of the end centers by drawing crossed diagonals, and mount it securely on the lathe. Bring the tool rest up to the work, turn the wood over by hand, just to make sure that it spins freely, and switch on the power.

Take the gouge of your choice and start by clearing away the waste and turning the wood down to a rough cylinder. This done, take the skew chisel, rest the bevel on the wood, angle the blade slightly to start the cut, and make a clean unbroken pass along the length of the workpiece. Work from one end to the other, then flip the skew chisel over and work back. Repeat this procedure until you have cleared away the rough. Then set the calliper to the required diameter, and continue turning until you reach the desired calliper reading. Aim for a cylinder diameter of about two inches.

Woodturning Tip

As to the question of whether or not you should switch off the power when using callipers, I say that if you are confident and experienced, then there's no reason at all why you shouldn't take the calliper readings while the wood is spinning. But, then again, if you are a cautious beginner, then it's always a good idea to switch off before taking readings.

Setting Out the Design and Stepping the Waste

Once you have turned the wood down to a smooth cylinder, take the dividers and set out all the step-offs that make up the design (see 9–2, left). Working from left to right along the cylinder, allow two inches for the headstock/chuck waste, 1½ inch for the bobbin/ball, ¼ inch for parting waste, 2¼ inches for the main whorl, two inches for the spindle, ½ inch for the finial at the top of the spindle, and, lastly, ½ inch for tailstock waste.

Having clearly marked out all the step-offs with the points of the dividers, then take the callipers and the parting tool, and sink pilot cuts to establish the largest diameters of the various component parts. Working from left to right along the workpiece, aim for a cylinder diameter of 1½ inches for the bobbin, 2¼ inches for the whorl, ⅜ inch for the spindle, and about ⅞ inch for the finial. Mark each cylinder off with two or more pilot cuts—one at each end and maybe another in the middle. So, for example, if we take it that you are starting out with an overall cylinder diameter of two inches, then, to achieve the 1½-inch diameter for the bobbin, you will have to run the parting tool to a depth of ¼ inch. And then again, when you come to the spindle at ⅜-inch diameter, you will have to run the pilot cuts to a depth of a little over ¾ inch. I usually describe the diameter at the bottom of the pilot cuts, as being the diameter at the "core" (see 9–3).

When you are satisfied with the depth of the cuts and the resultant calliper readings—meaning the readings at

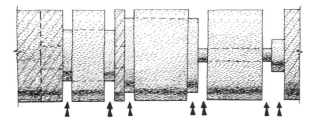

9–3 Establish the largest diameter of the various component parts by using the parting tool to sink pilot cuts. Note how each step, or diameter, is set out with two such cuts.

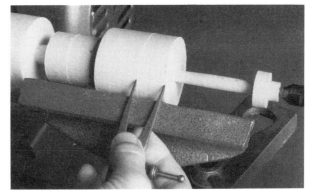

9–4 Use the dividers to set the turning out with additional guidelines—lines that mark the position of the largest diameter.

the core—then take the skew chisel, and turn the waste down to achieve the desired stepped core diameters. It is best to minimize the risk of knocking the workpiece off center by working from the tailstock end to the headstock. First remove the bulk of the waste from around the spindle, then work the whorl, and so on, along the length of the wood. The working process is wonderfully simple and straightforward, all you do is swiftly turn down the waste until you are within a whisker of the level of the pilot cuts, and then turn the stepped cylinder to a good finish. When you have realized the diameters of the bobbin, whorl, spindle, and finial, take the dividers and carefully set out three guideline step-offs—one halfway along the bobbin, another about ¾ inches down from the top of the whorl, and a third to split the width of the finial (see 9–4).

Lastly, with the guidelines in place, take the parting tool, and sink the parting-off waste—at head and tail, and between the bobbin and the main whorl—to a depth of ¾ inch. Aim to be left with a central core about ½ inch in diameter (see 9–5).

Turning the Bobbin Whorl and Finial

When you have achieved the stepped form, set out the guidelines, and have defined the three parting-off points, then take the skew chisel and set to work turning all of the curves, beads, and shoulders that make up the design.

Start by raising the tool rest so that it is slightly above the center-of-spin height. This done, rest the flat blade on the workpiece so that the heel is "looking" in the direction of the cut, and then carefully draw the chisel back towards your body until the heel part of the bevel rubs and bites into the wood. When you feel the tool begin to bite, slide-and-guide the chisel at a steady even pace along the workpiece. A good working action is to press the chisel blade hard-down with the thumb of one hand, while at the same time guiding and pushing the handle with the other (see 9–6).

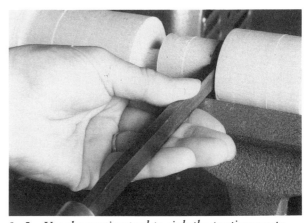

9–5 Use the parting tool to sink the parting waste.

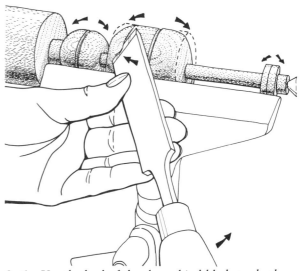

9–6 Use the heel of the skew chisel blade to do the cutting.

The knack of using a skew chisel is in knowing just how to angle the shaft of the chisel, and when to lift up the handle so that the blade bevel bites and cuts. The encouraging news is that you can easily tell if you are doing it right; you will be producing long shavings rather than dust and debris.

Woodturning Tip

The great thing about woodturning is that there are just about as many ways of getting a job done as there are woodturners. One woodturner will use a skew chisel this way, and another will do it that way, and so on. The only problem is that some raw beginners are worried that there isn't a single sure route. My advice, is to try out the various ways, and then select the one that works for you.

When you have a good understanding of how best to use the skew chisel—and this could take you anything from ten days to ten years (I'm *still* learning)—then set to work turning the profiles to shape. Starting with the bobbin, and being mindful to work from high wood down to low wood, set the heel of the skew chisel down on the central guideline, and cut out-and-down to round-over the shoulder of the cylinder. Make repeated cuts—down-and-over on one side of the guideline, and then down-and-over on the other side, until the ball-like bobbin begins to take shape. Don't worry too much if the bobbin is not quite ball shaped, just do your best to aim for a ball—then you can happily settle for something else. If you aren't too comfortable using the skew chisel, then try using a square-ended chisel, or even a ¼-inch- or ⅜-inch-wide, long round-nosed gouge.

With the bobbin turned to shape, then repeat the procedures to turn the whorl and the finial at the top of the spindle. The mistake many beginners make is to hold the tool with an iron-like grip and try to bully the wood to shape. The secret of success is not to force the tools, but rather to ease up on any tendency to have a vice-like grip, to hold the chisel or gouge in a more-relaxed manner, and to let the carefully angled tool do the work. If you get the angle and thrust of the bevel on the wood right, then the rest will follow.

DECORATING, POLISHING, AND PARTING OFF

Having turned what you consider is a good string of components, use the skew chisel to turn the decorative V-cuts—around the whorl and the bobbin. Use the toe of the tool, and aim for a cut about ⅛ inch wide and ⅛ inch deep. This done, stay with the parting tool—or you

9–7 *You can use the edge of an old tool to friction-burn the decorative rings.*

might use an old tool or a length of wire—and press down hard to friction-burn decorative lines—one on each side of the V-cuts and one around the median of the finial. If you use the parting tool, then make the burn with one of the sharp edges (see 9–7).

Technique and Safety of Using Wire for Decorative Burning

If you decide to use a length of wire to make the decorative burn, then there are a couple of do's and don'ts to bear in mind.
- Don't have the wire so short that it gets hot and burns your hands.
- Do be mindful that a long length of wire wrapped around your hands/fingers is not a good idea since there is a danger of your hands and the wire getting snagged, and the ends of the wire flying round and cutting you, especially your face.
- Don't pull so hard on the wire that you jerk the workpiece off center.

Take the stick of carnauba wax and rub it firmly on the spinning workpiece. Not so hard mind you that a shell of wax builds up, but just enough to cover the wood in a light skim. This done, take a small tight pad of cloth—it could be felt, cotton, or wool—and hold it hard on the spinning workpiece until the heat built up by the friction drives the wax into the surface of the wood (see 9–8). Work systematically backwards and forwards along the work until you achieve an agreeable high-gloss finish. Do this along the entire string of turnings.

9–8 *Having rubbed on the carnauba wax, use a pad of cloth to burnish the surface to a high-gloss finish.*

Woodturning Polishing Tip

If you don't like the hard shine of carnauba wax, then consider using beeswax—or even furniture wax.

Parting Off and Drilling Holes

Take the skew chisel, turn it over so that the long point or toe is at the bottom, and then, working from the tailstock end to the chuck, carefully bring the components to a well-turned, clean finish, and part off. Bearing in mind that the workpiece needs to be held secure in a chuck— we use a four-jaw chuck—the procedure is to bring the finial to a good finish and part off the tail-center waste, and then turn the spindle off from the top of the whorl, and so on. It's all simple enough as long as the chisel is sharp and the wood is well secured and stable. When you are nipping off the spindle from the whorl, run the point of the skew chisel deep into the whorl to make a good clear guide mark for the drill bit. Be sure to bring the bottom of the whorl—the part of the spinning top that's going to be doing the spinning—to a pointed finish. It should be not so sharp that the point is going to crumble away, nor so rounded that there's a large point-of-spin area, just a clean point—like the point on a lemon.

With the three components nicely finished and parted off—the spindle complete with finial, the whorl, and the bobbin—take the bobbin and rub down two opposite side-faces. Cut the 1½ inch diameter down to a thickness of about ⅞ inch.

Take the bobbin, whorl, and spindle to the bench drill press, and set out all the bits in readiness. When you have checked and double-checked that all is correct, support and control the whorl in a jig, like an egg in a cup (see 9–9, left). Start by boring a ⅜-inch-diameter hole about ½ inch straight down into the top center—the little dip left by the point of the chisel. Next, having worked out how to hold the workpiece securely, bore two holes through the bobbin—a ½-inch-diameter hole through the north–south axis (see 9–9, top right), and a ¾-inch-diameter hole through the side. Position the side hole so that it runs in through the middle of one flat face and out though the other, and so that it runs at right angles through the north-south hole (see 9–9, bottom).

Slide the bobbin on the spindle, push it up to within about ¼ inch of the finial, and then take a pencil and carefully mark a middle-of-bobbin-hole point—for the string hole—on the spindle. Refer to the working drawing details (see 9–2, bottom).

Finally, when you are pretty sure that all is correct, remove the bobbin for a moment, and bore a 1/16-inch-diameter hole through the spindle.

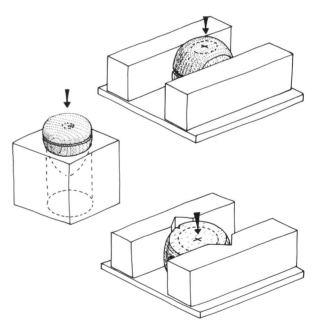

9–9 *(Left) Hold the whorl securely in a drilled out piece of waste wood, and bore a ⅜-inch-diameter hole down into the top center. (Top right) With the wood held securely, bore a ½-inch-diameter hole through the north–south axis. (Bottom right) Secure the workpiece between a couple of easy-to-make V-blocks—so that it is flat-face uppermost—and bore a ¾-inch diameter hole through the center of one flat face and out the other.*

PUTTING TOGETHER AND FINISHING

Start by having a trial assembly. Slide the spindle through the ½-inch bobbin hole, and push it for a tight fit into the top of the whorl. Push the spindle down into the whorl, until there is a gap of about 1½ inches between the whorl and the finial, and until the spindle string hole is centered on the ¾-inch-diameter through-bobbin hole. The proportions and positions have to be correct; so spend time getting everything right. As needed, trim the spindle to length and/or reposition the string hole. Once everything seems about right, wedge the spindle tight with a tiny splint of wood, and knot the pull-string through the spindle.

Assembly Tip

It's most important that the spindle be aligned with the axis of the whorl. To this end, ask a friend to line it up in one direction, while you line it up in another.

And now for the big test! With the string knotted in the hole, wound around the spindle, and knotted at the pull-end, hold the bobbin between thumb and index finger, and, at one and the same time, pull and let go of the string. Meaning that you hold onto the bobbin and let the string go. If all is well, and the top is spinning, set it down carefully on a level worksurface—and let go of the bobbin.

When you have achieved a top that spins, remove the splint wedge, clean wax off the end of the spindle, cut a small slot for glue, and dribble a small amount of Super Glue down the spindle and into the whorl hole.

Lastly—and this is the most difficult bit—present the spinning top to your favorite kid, give them a wow-isn't-this-great demonstration, and leave them to it!

TROUBLESHOOTING AND POSSIBLE MODIFICATIONS

- If you are working on a very small lathe, then it might be as well to make the project as three separate between-center turnings.
- If you like the idea of the project, but want to play around with the design and techniques, you could, perhaps, turn the whorl and spindle all-of-a-piece so that the spindle is part of the whorl, slide the bobbin on the spindle, and hold it in place with a bead for a finial. This way of working ensures a perfectly aligned spindle.
- You could also modify the design so that the spindle passes right on through the whorl—so that the end of the spindle becomes the point-of-spin.
- If you want to go for a fancier top, you could fit it out with a brass round-head nail for the point-of-spin and, maybe, stain it with colored inks.

· 10 ·

German Nutcracker Soldier

A nut-cracking machine in the shape of a nineteenth-century German soldier—a traditional Christmas toy

As I remember, when we gave one of our sons a nutcracker toy for Christmas, his first comment went something like, "Yuck, what a weird and gross thing!" And he was quite right—traditional nutcracker figures are both unusual and somewhat grotesque. With their big snarly-toothed nutcracker mouths, hooked noses, wild hair, long beards, and fierce expressions, they are, in many ways, a curious and rather sinister toy.

At an earlier time, after I had taken one of these figures to bits and discovered how it worked, I became so intrigued by the whole notion of nutcracker figures that I decided to find out a little bit about their origins—where, when, and why they were first made.

In Germany—in the eighteenth and nineteenth century—a traditional Christmas was celebrated by eating lots of fancy foods including gingerbread figures, sugar pretzels, and real nuts that had been both painted and gilded. It followed that if you want to eat a nut, then you first have to break open the hard shell. And this is where nutcracker soldiers march in (see 10–1). As far as I can make out, nutcracker figures—soldiers, gendarmes, Prussian generals, and kings—sometimes called gobblers—have a tradition, that goes back at least as far as the sixteenth century, when they were made in such places as Sonneberg and Berchtesgaden.

The wooden nutcrackers were all part and parcel of Christmas Day—along with the traditional elements of decorating a tree, Father Christmas, the Yule log, and all the rest. They were given as presents to accompany the nuts and other goodies. The idea was that after Christmas—when all the nuts had been eaten—the figures ceased being strictly functional and became playthings, like dolls and toy soldiers.

In the nineteenth century, a certain Ernst Theodor Amadeus Hoffmann built on the nutcracker tradition when he wrote his now famous fairy tale "The Nutcracker and The Mouse King." And last but not least, we are all probably familiar with Tchaikovsky and his much loved ballet "The Nutcracker Suite."

From a woodturning viewpoint, the nutcracker figure is a really good introduction to the art of making toys that have hinged and pivoted movement—such as dolls, marionette puppets, and music box automatons.

If you relish making complex turned toys, and if you like the challenge of putting lots of small well-matched parts together, then this project is going to provide you with a great deal of finger-tingling pleasure.

10–1   Project picture.

THOUGHTS ON DESIGN AND TECHNIQUE

After you have had a good, long look at the project picture (see 10–1), and maybe even visited craft shops and museums to see traditional German nutcrackers in "person," have a look at the working drawings (see 10–2 and 10–3).

Toymaking Tip

If you reckon to make a lot of woodturned toys, then it's a good idea to keep an "ideas sketchbook" or scrap book. We have a collection of magazine cuttings, clips from museum hand-outs, sketches, notes on colors, advertisements for modern toys, and so on. It's all good source material.

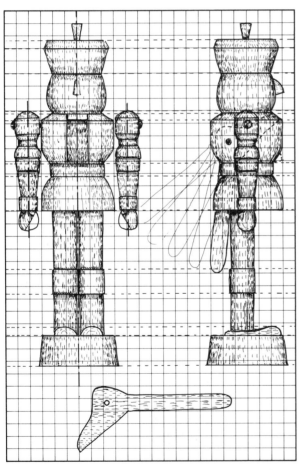

10–2 Working drawings—at a scale of two grid squares to one inch, the finished soldier stands about 14 inches high and is almost five inches across the span of the shoulders. Note the movement of the lever.

Note how the nine turned components—the head–hat, the torso, the two arms, the two legs, the two feet, and the base—are worked as three individual turnings (see 10–3). The head-hat and torso are worked as one turning, the limbs and feet as another, and the base is worked on its own. That said, if your wood supply is such that you want to make the head and hat as separate units, make the legs singly, or whatever, then fine; just be sure to modify the order of working accordingly.

So, for example, if you figure to turn the head and torso all-of-a-piece—as they appear on the finished soldier—then be aware that since the head is part of the body, you will have to cut the mouth-lever slot with a drill bit and chisel—like a mortise. But, then again, if you enjoy cutting mortises, that's just fine; such a procedure is probably the best way forward for you. In fact, I see from one traditional museum piece nutcracker to another that the turners have used all manner of making and putting-together options. Much depends on whether or not you are actually going to be cracking nuts! I say this, because if you feed the soldier lots of nuts—in which case you will be pushing the lever hard against the head—then it might be a good idea to prevent the nutcracker losing his head by turning the head and body all-of-a-piece. Decide for yourself what you want to do.

Have a look at the working drawings (see 10–2), and consider how the lever is fitted and pivoted within the body slot in such a way that the top end of the lever becomes the bottom jaw, while the bottom end becomes the tail of the soldier's coat. Look ahead to the painting grid (refer to 10–22), and note the way that the beard conceals the slot underneath the jaw, while the long hair covers up the slot at the back of the body. The arms are pivoted with brass screws rather than being dowelled and glued in place. With traditional nutcrackers the arms are usually a glued fixture, but our thinking was that as the kids are only going to try and pivot the arms anyway—with the effect that as like as not they will break off—then it might be best to build a pivot-arm feature into the project.

Finally, consider how we have gone for traditional imagery with the red coat, crossed braids, and the grim and growly gnashing expression.

Woodturning Tip

And why, you might ask, do we prefer to use a four-jaw chuck, rather than one with three-jaws, or even one of the new specials? Well . . . the answer is wonderfully simple. The four-jaw function, means that you can grip a piece of square-section wood right from the start, without the need to first turn the end down to a round section.

Lathe and Tool Considerations

As always, we endorse using a four-jaw chuck, if for no other reason than that once the workpiece is held in the jaws and pivoted at the tailstock, then you can be pretty certain that the wood is going to stay put.

If you want to work without a chuck, or if your funds don't include a chuck, then there's no reason at all why this project can't be turned between centers—meaning between a pronged center at the headstock and a live/plain center at the tailstock.

As for special tools, we have chosen to use a coping saw for cutting the lever slot and a scroll saw for cutting the lever. You could use a coping saw for both tasks.

Tools and Equipment

Apart from a lathe, you need—
- round-nosed gouge
- parting tool
- skew chisel
- scroll saw
- coping saw
- ¼-inch chisel
- bench or hand drill with a ¼-inch drill bit
- both dividers and callipers
- pencil and ruler
- sheet each of tracing and workout paper
- pack of graded sandpapers

- Super Glue
- two soft-haired watercolor paintbrushes—a broad and a fine point
- acrylic paints in the colors red, beige, yellow, green, brown, gold, blue, white, and black
- small quantity of clear varnish
- small piece of real fur or fur fabric for the beard and hair
- two roundhead brass screws at about 1½ inches long

Wood

For this project you need a 10-inch length of easy-to-turn wood three by three inches square for the hat–head and body, a 32-inch length of easy-to-turn wood at 1½ inches square, for the limbs and feet, a four-inch length of three by three inch square-section of wood for the base, and a ¾-inch-thick plank of wood about four inches wide and eight inches long for the lever and bottom jaw.

As for the wood type, much depends on whether or not you want to use the nutcracker actually to crack nuts. If you do, select a hard wood like beech, and if you don't, then use a soft wood like lime or jelutong.

In the context of toymaking, you do have to be alert to the fact that, since the wood is likely to be much handled and even sucked and chewed by children, it must be completely splinter resistant, colorfast, and nontoxic. If you have any doubts, then talk to a specialist wood supplier.

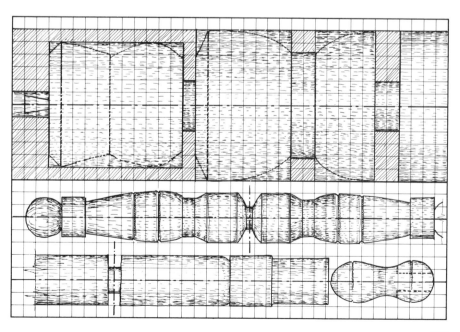

10–3 Working drawings—the scale is four grid squares to one inch. The turning order is—(top) head and body, (middle) arms, (bottom) legs and foot/feet.

TOYMAKING STAGES

Making the Hat, Head, and Body—Setting Out the Wood and First Cuts

Look closely at the working drawings (see 10–2 and 10–3), and draw the nutcracker at full size. Take the 10-inch length of three by three inch square-section wood, establish the end centers by drawing crossed diagonals, and secure it on the lathe. Tighten up the chuck key, wind up the tailstock, set the tool rest a little below the center of spin, and generally make ready for turning.

Woodturning Tip

It's always a good idea before switching on the power to turn the wood over by hand, just to make sure that the spinning wood isn't going to strike the tool rest. Be aware that, although the height is variable and depends on the type, size, and use of such-and-such a tool, the tool rest always needs to be as close as possible to the workpiece—without actually touching.

10–4 *At one and the same time, use the callipers to measure the depth of the parting-tool cut and the diameter of the resultant core.*

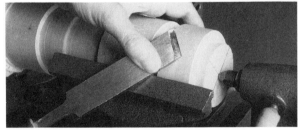

10–5 *Press the skew chisel bevel-down onto the workpiece, and cut the steps down to the depth of the guide cuts.*

When you are happy that all is correct, switch on the power, and use the gouge to swiftly turn the wood down to a round section. Aim for a diameter that is as near as possible to three inches. With the wood accurately turned down to a cylinder, take the ruler and divider, and set out all the step-offs that make up the design. Working from left to right along the wood, and allowing a small amount for chuck waste, step off ½ inch for the hat plume, 1¼ inch for the hat, 1½ inches for the head/face, ¼ inch for waste, two inches for the chest, ½ inch for the belt, 1½ inches for the hips, and the remainder for tailstock waste. Check and double-check all the measurements.

With all the "length" step-offs carefully set out—the length of the hat, the length of the face, and so on—then comes the sometimes tricky procedure of turning each of the step-offs down to the desired diameter. I say "sometimes tricky," because many beginners are not comfortable using the calliper and the parting tool at one and the same time to cut the depth guides. In fact, the procedure is beautifully simple and direct as long as you take it easy and work at a controlled pace.

Woodturning Safety Tip

If you are at all worried about using the calliper in this way, then bring the wood to a stand-still before taking each reading.

Start by establishing the largest diameter of the part that needs to be turned. So, for example—with the hat—although the cone-like hat tapers from top to bottom, the greatest diameter is 2½ inches. This being so, set the calliper to a fraction over 2½ inches, then take the parting tool and sink a couple of ¼-inch deep depth guides on the hat section so that you are left with a central core of 2½ inches. What we usually do is run the tool into the wood, to within about 1/16 inch of the required diameter, then set the callipers on the spinning workpiece, while at the same time also cutting the guide slot deeper (see 10–4). When the callipers slip over the wood, then the cut is complete. Continue working along the wood, cutting two depth/guide slots for each step-off.

Having fixed the core diameters, take the round-nosed gouge or the skew chisel, and cut the steps down to match up with the depth guides (see 10–5). Next, take the divider, and mark on the wood any guidelines that you consider will help you on your way—perhaps with the curves or maybe with the painting, or even with the position of secondary "valleys." For example, we set-in a line ¼-inch down from the top of the hat to fix the

10–6 Label the finished steps so that you know exactly where you are.

position of the greatest diameter, another one ¼ inch down from the top of the body to fix the position of the shoulders, another one 1¼ inches down from the very top of the hat to fix the "valley" where the hat meets the head, and so on (see 10–6).

Cutting the Profile Curves

When you have achieved all the steps and diameters that make up the design, and when you have set-in as many guidelines as you think necessary, then take the large skew chisel, and set to work turning all the curves and faces (see 10–7). So, for example, with the hat–head, all you do is nip in the angle at the top of the hat, run a slope "downhill" towards the head, turn the head down to a ball shape, and so on along the length of the figure.

Woodturning Guidelines

It's all pretty straightforward as long as you try to follow a few simple rules of thumb. If you are new to wood-turning, then it is best to think of these rules as being your own personal dos and don'ts.

- Do make sure that your tools are sharp.
- Don't try to cut "up hill" against the grain.
- Do use the heel of the skew chisel when you are turning down a curve.
- Don't rush the final stages.
- Do keep adjusting the tool rest so that it is as close as possible to the work.

   If you keep making the same mistakes—I do!—then take note, and add another do/don't to your list.

Once you have achieved the shape of the hat, head, and body, skim the surface to a final finish, and rub down with fine-grade sandpaper. Turn the skew chisel so that the toe is pointed downwards, and set-in selected V-cuts to crisp up the design (see 10–8 and 10–9). Finally, part-off the wood from the tailstock, part-off the body from the head, and part-off the hat–head from the chuck waste.

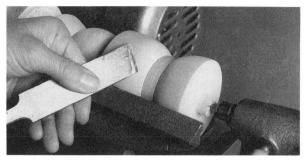

10–7 Angle the heel of the skew chisel until it begins to bite, and then—working downhill—turn the wood down to the desired profile.

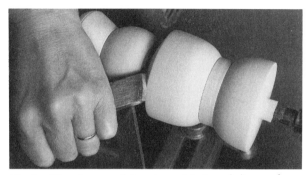

10–8 Use the toe of the skew chisel to define and set-in the V-cuts.

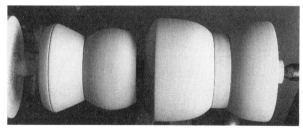

10–9 The completed hat–head and body sections are ready to be parted-off.

Turning the Arms, Legs, and Feet

Turning the string of components that make up the limbs and the feet uses much the same procedure as already described for the hat–head and body. Set the wood in the lathe, turn it down to the greatest diameter needed, use the divider to set out the step-offs, lower the step-offs, use the skew chisel to turn the individual components to shape, and so on. That said, you do have an added complication, in that, you are trying to try make matching pairs—two arms, and two legs. The feet are actually a single turning that is split/sawn from end to end. You could cut a cardboard template, but I find that the best strategy is to turn the matching pairs off as mirror-imaged twins (refer to 10–3). So for instance, if you look ahead at the photographs (refer to 10–11), you will see that with the two arms, the shoulders are together, and with the legs, the two hips are touching. The idea is that as you are turning off the matched pair, you can skip backwards and forwards from one to the other, always aiming to keep the total two-piece turning symmetrical—like a bow tie or the wings of a butterfly. It is an unnecessary and big mistake to try making matching pairs one at a time, or even to set them out so that they run shoulder to fist, shoulder to fist.

Woodturning Tip

When you are working long thin spindles—especially where areas are much reduced in diameter—you will have to support both the wood and the tool (see 10–10).

Once you have turned off the string of components, use the toe of the skew chisel to set-in all of the V-cuts that make up the design. The procedure is to turn the chisel over so that the toe edge is pressed firmly down on the

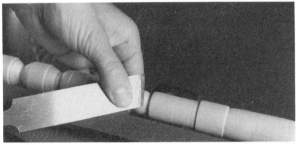

10–10 *At one and the same time, cradle the spindle with your fingers, and use your thumb to press down on the skew chisel.*

10–11 *Advance the toe of the skew chisel so that it makes a cut, and then twist it slightly left-and-right to complete the V-section.*

tool rest, hold the handle down so that the toe is pointing at the workpiece, advance the chisel so that it makes a cut, and, lastly, tidy up the V-section by twisting the chisel slightly left (see 10–11).

Finally, give the string of turnings a brisk rub down with fine-grade sandpaper, remove them from the lathe, and use a fine-blade saw to cut them into separate components.

Making the Base

Take the four-inch length of three-by-three-inch square-section wood, mount it securely in the four-jaw chuck, and spend time running through your pre-switch-on safety list. Switch on the power and get to work. Take a gouge—I use a round nosed—and swiftly turn the wood down to the largest possible round section. This done, take the parting tool, and run a parting cut to a depth of about one inch—to establish the base line. Have the cut as close as you safely can to the chuck.

After you have turned down a cylinder and cut in a base line, then reduce the sides slightly so that the base tapers from top to bottom (see 10–12). Be mindful that the base has to be large enough for the two feet to be set side by side.

With the sides nicely tapered, move the tool rest so that it is over the bed of the lathe, and use the round-nosed gouge and the skew chisel to true-up what will be the top or face of the base (see 10–13). Making sure that the rest is set more or less square with the workpiece, take the gouge, enter it in from the side, and clear the face from side to the middle. Skim the face of the wood down to a smooth finish by moving the tool in a little sweep. Take the skew chisel, or you might better use a square-ended scraper, and remove the little ripples as left by the gouge.

Having trued-up the face and tested the level with a metal straightedge, then give the whole workpiece a rub down with fine-grade sandpaper and part-off.

10–12 *Use the gouge to turn the tapered base.*

Making and Fitting the Jaw–Lever

Now for the best bit of all—the bit we have all been waiting for—the putting together.

To recap—you should have eight turned pieces in all; the hat–head, the torso, two legs, two arms, a single "foot" piece which is going to be cut end-to-end to make two feet, and the base. Before you go any further, trace the shape of the bottom jaw lever from your working drawing (see 10–2), pencil-press the profile to your piece of ¾-inch thick wood—so that the grain runs down the length of the handle—and cut it out on the scroll saw (see 10–14, left). Rub the cut faces down to a smooth, slightly round-edged finish, and put it to one side.

Take the torso, arrange the grain to best advantage, label it "top," "bottom," "front" and "back"—just so that you know what goes where—and run a midline down and around the whole piece. With the divider set to ⁷⁄₁₆ inch, and starting at the top front edge of the belt, prick out a series of guide marks that run on either side of the midline. Work up the front of the chest, over the neck, and down to the bottom of the hips to finish up with a "track" that measures about ⁷⁄₈ inch wide. Shade in the track with pencil (see 10–14, right).

Now for the difficult bit! Set the torso top-side-up in a muffled vise, take the coping saw, and make two parallel cuts straight down from the neck and through to the top of the belt (see 10–15, left).

Woodturning Tip

If you aim to do a lot of turning, then it is a good idea to grip the round-section wood in sets of easy-to-make V-blocks. V-blocks are wonderful for holding and controlling round sections.

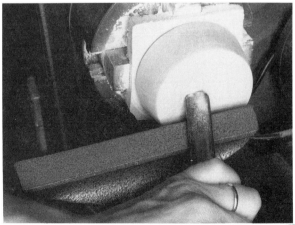

10–13   Use the tool of your choice to true-up the top face of the base.

With the cuts set a little to the waste side of the drawn line—so that the finished channel measures just a smudge over ¾ inch wide—link them at the top-of-the-belt line so that the slice of waste falls away. Next, reposition the torso in the vise so that the "back" is uppermost and so that the "bottom" end is nearest to you, and make two saw cuts down from the top of the belt to the bottom of the hips. Make the cuts to a depth of about ½ inch.

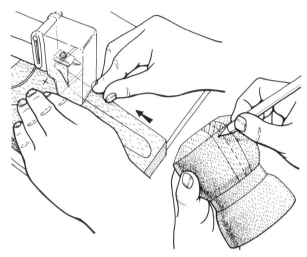

10–14   (Left) Use the scroll saw to fret out the shape of the ¾-inch-thick jaw lever. (Right) Shade in the area of waste to establish the width and position of the jaw "track."

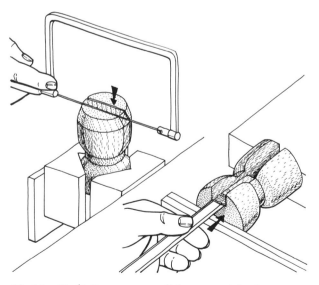

10–15   (Left) Run two parallel cuts straight down from the neck through to the top of the belt. (Right) Take the ½-inch-wide chisel and use small, tight controlled strokes to skim away the waste.

The next bit isn't so easy; so spend time getting it right. With the torso still secured in the vise, take your ½-inch wide chisel, and very carefully lower the belt-to-bottom channel to a depth of about ½ inch. Skim away the waste with small, tightly controlled cuts, being very careful not to let the chisel slip or to run into the wood at the side of the channel (see 10–15, right).

When you have sliced out the channel, take the lever, and have a trial fitting. If needs be—if its too tight a fit—use a piece of sandpaper and a block to rub the inside faces down to a smooth finish.

Study the working drawings (refer to 10–2), so that you know precisely where the pivot hole needs to be located; then slide the lever in place, and strap it securely with elastic bands. Cradle the workpiece between a couple of pieces of waste—or you might use a V-block—and run a ¼-inch-diameter hole through the side of the body, through the lever, and into the wood at the other side. Remove all the bands, and have a trial fitting with a length of ¼-inch dowel (see 10–16 and 10–17). Ideally the dowel needs to be a tight fit in the body holes, and an easy, loose fit through the lever.

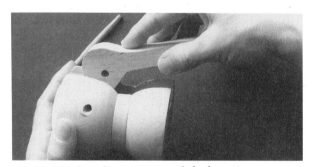

10–16 *Make adjustments until the lever is an easy fit.*

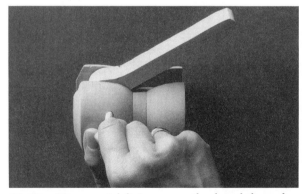

10–17 *Have a trial fitting—run the dowel through the side of the body, through the lever, and into the other side of the body.*

Finally, once you are pleased with the overall fit, remove the dowel and have a swift rub down with sandpaper.

FITTING THE HEAD, ARMS, LEGS, AND FEET

Before you do anything else, take the single "foot" turning, and run it through the scroll saw so that you have two little foot shapes. If you are at all worried about the idea of pushing such a small turning straight through the saw—you might cut your fingers—then play it safe and work from end to middle (see 10–18, top left and right). When you have achieved the two half-turnings, sand the sawn faces to a smooth finish (see 10–18, bottom).

Sanding Block Tip

To make a "rubbing down" surface take a sheet each of sandpaper and plywood, set them together so that the sandpaper is grit-side-up, and fix them with strips of double-sided sticky tape (refer to 10–18, bottom).

Pencil-label the head, arms, legs and feet "front," "left," and "right," so that you know with certainty what goes where and how.

Take the two arms, mark the pivot points on the side of the "shoulders," and bore through them with the ¼-inch drill. Rub the exit holes down so that there is a slight flatness, and screw the arms in place on the torso. Be very careful that the screws don't run into the lever slot. Next, have another trial fitting with the lever, just to make sure that it's still a smooth, easy fit.

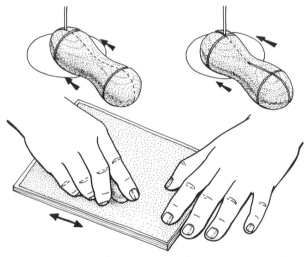

10–18 *(Top) Push the turning through to the half-way point, and then change ends to complete the cut. (Bottom) Set the sanding surface grit-side-up, and rub the sawn faces down to a smooth finish.*

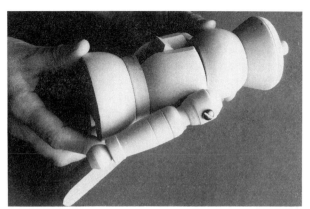

10–19   Glue the head onto the shoulders.

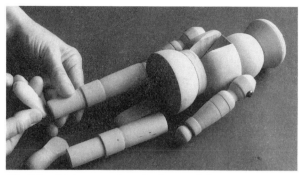

10–20   Make sure that the legs and feet come together for an accurate fit.

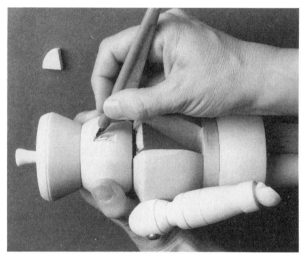

10–21   Use the craft knife to shape the nose and to cut the mortise hole.

With the arms and lever in place, dribble a generous amount of Super Glue on the top of the torso and on the bottom of the head, and fit the two together (see 10–19).

Take the feet, and use the chisel and sandpaper to level the back-top surface—meaning where the foot joins the legs. Lower the wood at the back of each foot until the legs and the feet come together for an accurate flush fit (see 10–20).

Continue trimming and sanding the feet and the ends of the legs until you are able to stand the nutcracker up without it toppling over. Spend time getting everything just right—the height of the boots, the thickness of the feet, the height of the legs, and so on. When you have brought all the components together for what you deem is a good fit, glue them with Super Glue. What we did was glue and pin the feet on the base block, tap pins into all the other mating surfaces, clip the heads off the pins with a pair of pliers, and then work up from the bottom, gluing and locating until the job was done.

Sand the inside part of each ball-shaped hand to a flat-faced finish, cut the little stylized thumb nick with a penknife, cut, shape, mortise and glue-fit the little wedge nose (see 10–21), and generally tidy up all the loose ends. Finally, clear away all the dust and debris in readiness for painting or move to your dust-free area.

FINISHING AND PAINTING

And at last—the very exciting and satisfying task of painting! Have a good look at the project photograph (refer to 10–1), and the painting grid (see 10-22), and observe how we have stayed with traditional colors and imagery. We used bright red for the jacket and tail-lever, black with gold trim for the hat and boots, gold trim on the jacket, yellow trousers, beige-colored face, pink cheeks and nose, and so on.

With your painting area ready to go, unscrew the arms, unpeg the lever, and arrange the components for painting. What we did was push three thumb tacks into the base so that the nutcracker stood clear of the work surface, and we spiked the arms and the lever on splints of wood supported in Plasticine.

Start by laying on the large areas of ground color—the black hat, the beige-colored face, the red jacket, arms and lever, and so on. Next, when the ground paint is completely dry, take a fine-point paintbrush and bring out the secondary details—the gold trim on the hat, coat and boots, the white teeth, and so forth down the length of the figure. And, of course, if along the way, you have an urge to personalize the imagery by painting in medals, buttons, or whatever, then all to the good.

When the paint is completely dry, give the whole figure a couple of coats of clear high-gloss varnish, and put it to one side until dry.

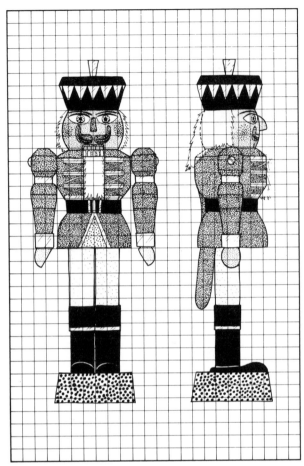

10–22 *Painting grid—the scale is two squares to one inch.*

Having already noted how the hair needs to be trimmed so that it hangs down over the lever slot at the back of the figure, and how the beard is stuck to the bottom jaw so that it hangs down over the lever slot at the front, cut the fur fabric to shape and glue it in place.

Finally, trim the hair and whiskers to their final shape, perhaps date and name the underside of the base, and then stand the nutcracker in pride of place, and wait for the requests for one just like it to come flooding in!

TROUBLESHOOTING AND POSSIBLE MODIFICATIONS

• The main difficulty with this project is not so much the turning, but rather how to cut the mouth/lever slot. The method you use to cut the slot, shapes the way the project is turned. For example, if you decide, say, to cut the slot with a drill and chisel—similar to a mortise—then you can turn the hat, head, and body all-of-a-piece.

• If you want to go for a super-strong nutcracking machine, then use a strong wood like beech, cut the mouth like a mortise, and have the legs glued and dowelled into the body.

• When we came to painting the finished project, we found that the wood—we used jelutong—sucked up the paint. It's a good idea, prior to painting, to seal the wood with a thin coat of varnish.

• Use a compass to set out the crown shape on the hat—set out the "points" with a series of compass step-offs.

• 11 •

Round-About

A round-about, turntable, or merry-go-round with six little figures and checkered tablecloth all set for tea

Kids have always enjoyed playing with very simple move-around toys—like merry-go-rounds, tinkle turn boxes, and turntables. A simple turntable on a spindle with a suggestion of animals or figures will keep little children amused for hours.

Our little merry-go-round (see 11–1) is the perfect plaything for a lively preschool toddler in that, not only is the movement very basic and easy to operate, but better still, the figures actually do move around the central table when the platform is turned. There aren't any springs to break or elastic mechanisms to fail, or anything else to endanger or frustrate the child—just a turntable that is hand-pushed around a central pivot, and six little "skittle" figures that sit in spigot holes. As to just what it is they are doing, we think of them as simply going round and round and round—just looking and waiting for their tea! But children with active imaginations will soon devise their own games—balancing the figures one on top of another, setting the table with candies, seeing how fast the figures can be spun around—there are any number of good-fun options.

As for the woodturning, we certainly don't want to leave you with the impression that the making is as easy as the playing—not a bit of it. This is a much more challenging project than it might at first seem. The discs need to be turned with precision and care, the figures need to have a crisp push-fit in the spigot holes, each of the figure designs needs to be slightly different, the spinning turntable must have a good fit with the central dowel, and so on.

If you enjoy working on a tight scale on a small lathe, and if have in mind a child who likes gentle, quiet fun, then this project is sure to be a high scorer.

THOUGHTS ON DESIGN AND TECHNIQUE

When you have assembled all your tools and materials, spend some more time looking at the project picture (see

11–1) and the working drawings (see 11–2), and generally understanding how the toy needs to be made and put together. Notice how the turntable is made up from four separate components—a base disc with a raised spigot or step at its middle, a rim-edged platform disc that is located on the base spigot, a spacer ring that sits at the middle of the platform, and the mushroom-like peg with its table-top imagery that runs through the other three components. Look closely at the cross-section detail on the working drawings (see 11–2, top), and see the way that the peg runs through both the spacer and the turntable platform to be glue-fixed in the base disc. Consider how for easy movement and assembly the various holes need to be slightly different diameters. The peg needs to pass through both the spacer ring and the turntable for a loose fit, while, at the same time, the end of the peg must be a tight, push-fit in the base hole.

The six spigot-bottomed figures sit in six location holes that are set equidistant around a circle in such a way that there is just enough space left between the sides of the figures and both the "mushroom" end of the peg and the rim of the turntable.

11–1   Project picture.

95

The height of the spigot or step at the middle of the base platform and the thickness of wood at the middle of the turntable allow both components to come together so that there is a space between the two of about ⅛ inch. This space is *critical*—it mustn't be so small that the two components scuff and grind together, nor so big that a small child can get his or her fingers stuck between them.

As for the imagery, we envisioned the figures as standing or sitting around a table and waiting for tea—hence the painted checkered table cloth. But you could just as well paint fairground animals and make it into a carousel, or have a pole in the middle instead of the mushroom peg as if the figures were dancing around a maypole or whatever. There are any number of interesting possibilities, but always be mindful of the dangers for little children of too-small an object, sharp or pointy bits, and any other hazard that you can think ahead about.

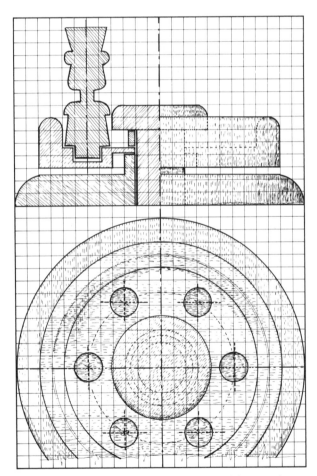

11–2 Working drawings—at a scale of four grid squares to one inch, the finished merry-go-round stands about three to four inches high and six inches wide. Note that there are two figure sizes.

Lathe and Tool Considerations

Although a wood-gripping chuck makes this project that much easier—for holding the turnings while you tidy up the tailstock end especially—there's nothing to say that you can't part-off in the usual manner and tidy up once the wood is off the lathe. You do, however, need a six-inch faceplate for the two discs, a good selection of large-diameter Forstner drill bits, and a drill press.

Tools and Equipment

Apart from a lathe, you need—
• six-inch faceplate
• square-end gouge, parting tool, and skew chisel
• bench drill press with Forstner bits two inches, one inch, and ½ inch in diameter
• both dividers and callipers
• pencil and ruler
• sheet each of tracing and workout paper
• pack of graded sandpapers
• Super Glue
• couple of soft-haired watercolor paintbrushes—a broad and a fine point
• acrylic paints in the colors red, white, light and dark blue, yellow, and green
• small quantity of clear varnish

Wood

We used jelutong for the discs, and beech for the figures. You will need—
• 1¼-inch-thick slab of easy-to-turn wood 6½ by 6½ inches square for the base disc
• 1¼-inch-thick wood slab 5½ by 5½ inches square for the turntable disc
• 4½-inch-square-length of wood 2½ by 2½ inches square for the middle "mushroom" pivot and the spacer ring
• two 12-inch lengths of wood 1½ by 1½ inches square for the six figures—two groups of three

TOYMAKING STAGES

Turning the Base Disc

Take the 1¼-inch-thick slab of jelutong 6½ by 6½ inches square—the piece for the base disc—and establish the center-point by drawing crossed diagonals on one square face. Draw a 6¼-inch-diameter circle with the compass, saw away the corners of waste, and screw the wood securely to the faceplate. Use short, fat screws that bite into the wood to a depth of no more than about ⅜ inch.

1₁–3 Having lowered the waste so that the spigot is standing in relief, use the toe of the skew chisel to clean out the angle at the step.

11–4 Turn down both sides of the high spot—at the top of the rim—to achieve the ½-inch half-round rim profile.

With the wood well mounted on the lathe, and having checked that you and the lathe are in good safe order, position the tool rest so that you can work the wood edge-on. Set out your tools so that they are comfortably at hand. Take the gouge, and start by swiftly turning the wood down to the largest possible diameter. Make short right-to-left sweeps, all the while, being very careful not to splinter the edge of the wood, and not to dull the edge of the gouge by catching it on the faceplate. Take the skew chisel—or you might use a parting tool or a scraper— and turn the edge of the wood down so that you have a clean-edged disc six inches in diameter. Having cleaned-up the edge of the disc, reposition the tool rest so that you can work the wood face-on, and use first the gouge and then the skew chisel to turn the face of the wood to a true, level finish. Lower the wood until the disc is one inch thick.

Once you have achieved the basic disc, set the dividers to a radius of ¾ inch, and scribe out a 1½-inch circle at its center. Take the parting tool, and sink a ⅜-inch-deep guide cut to the waste side of the circle—meaning to the outside of the scribed line. Working first with the gouge and then with the skew chisel carefully lower the face of the wood to the depth of the guide cut. Work from the middle to the side until you have a finished disc thickness of about ⅝ inch. Use the toe of the skew chisel to clean out the angle at the step (see 11–3).

To turn the quarter-circle profile/shoulder on the edge of the base, first set the dividers to a radius of ⅝ inch, and then scribe a line ⅝ inch from the outer edge. Don't cut too deeply, just enough to mark the surface. Next, take the tool of your choice—you could use a gouge or a skew chisel—and turn the edge of the disc down until you have a smooth-radius curve. Work the grain from high to low wood—that is, from the face of the disc over-and-round towards the edge (see 11–4).

Finally, give the whole workpiece a swift rub down with fine-grade sandpaper, and take it off the lathe.

Turning the Turntable

Take the 1¼ inch thick slab of 5½ by 5½ inch square wood, and mount it on the face plate, as already described. Turn down the edge and face, until you have a smooth one-inch-thick, five-inch-diameter square-edged disc. Use the divider to set out a line ½ inch in from the outer edge. Sink a ⅝-inch-deep guide cut, as already described for the base disc, only this time have the cut set to the waste side of the divider line so that you are left with a ½ thick rim running all the way around the edge. Once again, and still working with the gouge and the skew chisel, turn away the waste wood, so that the whole middle of the disc, from the center-point out to the rim, is lowered to a depth of ⅝ inch. You should be left with a thickness of no less than ⅜ inch.

With the middle of the disc cut away, take the skew chisel, and use the toe to set a "high-point" guideline ¼ inch in from the outer edge of the rim so that the ½-inch rim thickness is divided in half. To turn the curve of the rim, set the heel of the skew chisel flat-down on the high spot so that the heel is "looking" in the direction of the cut, and then, in a smooth, continuous rolling action, lift the handle until the blade begins to bite. Run the chisel over-and-in to cut away the sharp edge. Repeat this procedure on both sides of the high spot to achieve a ½-inch hemispherical profile. Lastly, clean up all the angles with the skew or the parting tool, rub down with sandpaper, and take the wood off the lathe.

Turning the Mushroom Peg and the Spacer Ring

Take the 4½-inch length of 2½ by 2½ inch square wood, establish the end center points by drawing crossed diagonals, and mount it securely on the lathe—in the chuck and pivoted at the tailstock. Turn the whole length of the wood down to a smooth two-inch diameter cylinder.

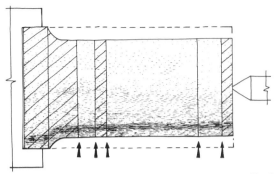

11–5 Use the ruler and the dividers to set out all of the step-offs that make up the design of the "mushroom" table and the spacer.

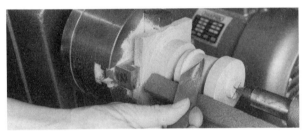

11–6 Use the gouge and the skew chisel to turn the stem down to a clean, one-inch diameter.

11–7 Part-off with the toe of the skew chisel—hold the workpiece and ease it gently backwards.

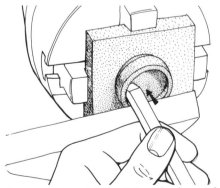

11–8 Turn out the middle of the cylinder so that the finished ring is a smooth, easy fit on the one-inch-diameter "mushroom" stem.

With the ruler and the divider, and, working from right to left along the cylinder, set out all of the step-offs that make up the design. Allow ¼ inch for tailstock waste, ½ inch for the mushroom top, two inches for the length of the stem, ¼ inch for between-turning waste, ⅜ inch for the spacer ring, and the remainder for chuck waste (see 11–5).

Having checked and double-checked that you haven't made a mess-up with the measurements, take the parting tool, and start by sinking the between-turning waste in to a depth of about ¾ inch. Aim to leave a central core of about ½ inch. Take the skew chisel, and lower the stem step-off to finish with a diameter of one inch (see 11–6). Roundover the shoulder of the mushroom, clean out the step angle, and generally turn the wood down to a good finish. Draw the tailstock center back out of the way, and move the tool rest over the bed of the lathe so that you can work the top of the mushroom "table" face-on. Use the skew chisel to skim the table top down to a good finish.

When you are happy with the turning, support it, and ease it away from you with one hand, nipping it off with the toe of the skew chisel (see 11–7). If you run the tool into the wood, while at the same time easing back on the workpiece, it will come away in your hand without the need for force or the risk of the tool jamming in the cut.

With the peg-turning out of the way, turn the remainder of the wood down to a diameter of about 1⅝ inch. Turn the middle of the cylinder so that it's going to be a loose fit with the one-inch-diameter mushroom stem (see 11–8), and part-off a ring that is about ⅜-inch wide.

Turning the Figures

Mount the first length of 1½ by 1½ inch square wood securely on the lathe, and, as already described in other projects, quickly turn it to a cylinder about 1¼ inches in diameter. Before you go any further, have another look at the working drawings (see 11–2, top), and see how the bottom of the figures are reduced in diameter to make a step or a spigot so that they will be a nice, push-fit in a ½-inch-diameter hole. Note the way that the body part of the figure—the skirt and shoulders—are kept to a maximum diameter of one inch so that, when the figures are sitting in place in their spigot holes, they are an easy fit between the edge of the rim and the side of the mushroom table. We have ever-so-slightly varied the height measurements and hat shapes to give each figure a slightly different character.

Study the painting grid (see 11–11), and, perhaps, draw a few different hat shapes of your own. Take first the gouge and then the skew chisel, and turn the wood

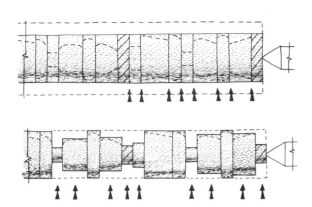

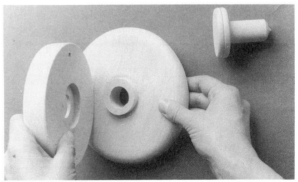

11–9 (Top) Step-off the measurements for the three small figures. (Bottom) Use the dividers and the parting tool to turn the wood down to a stepped profile.

down to a smooth, one-inch diameter. Next, take the divider and the ruler, and set out all of the step-offs that make up the design of the three small figures. From right to left along the cylinder allow ¼ inch for tailstock waste, ½ inch for the hat crown, ¼ inch for the hat brim, ½ inch for the face, ¼ inch for the neck, ¼ inch for the chest, ½ inch for the tummy, ⅝ inch for the hips, ¼ inch for the spigot, ¼ inch for between-figure waste (see 11–9, top), and so on along the length of the wood until you have three figures. And, of course, if, along the way you want to make the body step-offs shorter or whatever, just make any adjustments that you want.

After you have set out all of the step-off sizes that make up the three figures, take the divider and the parting tool, and turn the between-figure waste down to ⅜ inch, the spigots down to a diameter of ½ inch, the necks down to ¼ inch, the hat crowns down to ¾ inch, and so on (see 11–9, bottom). The only measurements that are really fixed are the ½-inch-diameter spigots, all of the others can be anything you fancy up to the maximum of one inch. Within these limitations, you can have a great time experimenting with tools and techniques.

With all of the step-offs cut to size, take the skew chisel, and set to work turning them to shape. Using the heel of the skew working from high to low wood, turn off just about whatever shape takes your fancy. We have gone for round edges for the hat brims, round cheeks, hat crowns that vary from being straight-sided to slightly rounded, rounded chests, tapered skirts, and so forth. The good thing about this project is that you can play around and create your own characters. Long, fat, straight-sided, tapered, bulgy-bodied, with hats tall, dumpy, conical, or squat; it makes no matter as long as you bear in mind that the spigots must be a good push-fit in the ½-inch-diameter holes.

Finally, when you have three nicely turned figures, rub them down with fine-grade sandpaper, and part them off from the lathe. Repeat the procedure for the other three figures.

DRILLING AND FITTING TOGETHER

Once you have turned all of the ten components—six figures, a base disc, the turntable, a spacer ring, and the mushroom peg—then comes the tricky task of boring out the various holes. Of course the actual drilling is easy enough, but the placing, the working sequence, and the alignment need careful consideration.

Starting with the base disc, all you need do is bore a single hole straight down through the middle of the stepped spigot to take the one-inch peg for a tight push-fit. As for the spacer ring, it needs to be a loose fit on the one-inch-diameter peg. You might have to rub down the hole and/or the peg, until the fit is just right.

When you come to the turntable disc, take the divider, set it to a radius of 1½ inches, and scribe a three-inch-diameter circle on the top, recessed surface. Step-off around the scribed circle, and make six arcs. Refer to the working drawings for details (refer to 11–2, bottom). Mark each of the six arc intersections into the wood to give a clear center point. Next, take the ½-inch drill bit, and bore out each of the six points to a depth of about ⅜ inch.

Set the turntable disc base–side uppermost on the bench drill press table, and fix the center point. Make two borings, a two-inch-diameter blind hole to a depth of about ¼ inch, and a one-inch-diameter hole that runs through the center of the two-inch diameter blind hole right through the wood.

Now comes the exciting bit of having a first dry-run assembly (see 11–10). Set the base disc flat-down, set the turntable in place on the spigot, place the spacer ring on

11–10 Have a trial fitting—set the turntable on the base, and fit the ring and stem.

99

11–11 Painting grid—the scale is four grid squares to one inch.

PAINTING AND FINISHING

Wipe all of the components with a damp cloth, and move to the dust-free area that you have set aside for painting. Study the painting grid once more (see 11–11). Bearing in mind that the close-fitting parts are best left unpainted—the spigots, the spigot holes, the spacer ring, and the stem of the peg—start by laying on the large areas of ground color. Our suggestion is to paint the base disc green, the turntable bright yellow, the "table cloth" white, and the figures red, white, and blue. We decided to give one figure a red hat, a blue top, and a red skirt, another figure a blue hat, a red top, and a white bottom, and so on with all six figures.

When the ground colors are dry, paint the crossed blue lines for the checkered table cloth, black for the hair, brows for eyes, red for the noses and mouths, and dark blue for the crossover squares on the light blue table cloth stripes. Wait awhile for the paint to dry, and then give everything, except the spigots and holes, a couple of coats of clear varnish.

Finally, reassemble the turntable, glue the mushroom table peg in place, make sure that the figures stand up both in their holes and on a flat surface, and give the merry-go-round a turn. The toy is ready and waiting for a fun-loving child.

TROUBLESHOOTING AND POSSIBLE MODIFICATIONS

- If you are lucky enough to have a tailstock drill chuck, then it's a good idea to bore out the main holes while the discs are in place on the lathe.
- When we came to painting the finished project, we found that the jelutong sucked up the paint. If you are using soft porous wood, it's a good idea, prior to painting, to seal it with a thin coat of varnish.
- When you are drilling large holes—meaning holes bigger than ½ inch—then make sure that the workpiece is held securely in a clamp or have a friend to help.
- On consideration, I would have made the turntable from thicker wood, the spigots longer, and the holes deeper. See what you think!

the turntable, and slide the mushroom peg through the hole. As needed, adjust the length of the peg so that the whole works comes together for a close, but easy, fit. If all is well, the table should turn, and everything else should stay put. While you are at it, test the figures in their holes, and make sure that they stand upright when they are on a level surface. As needed, dish (make concave) the underside of the spigots slightly so that the figures stand upright.

· 12 ·

Czechoslovakian Trumpet

A trumpet or horn in the shape of an old lady's head

When we were kids, way back in the 1950s, Christmas stocking-stuffer toys tended to be small, made from basic materials like wood, paper, and fabric, usually foreign in origin, and inexpensive. One Christmastime, my stocking contained a wooden yo-yo from Russia, a paper bird made in China, a wooden whip and top from Poland, and, best of all, a curious honking trumpet made in Czechoslovakia (see 12–1).

Part of the fun with toys of this character was exactly that they were so completely outside the normal run of things. They were packaged in strangely printed boxes—with lots of wrong spelling—and when I took them apart (I always wanted to know how they worked) they often contained unusual surprises. For example, we had a papier mâché toy from Germany that was made of pre World War II bank notes, and a whistle that looked to be made from a spent cartridge casing.

But, back to the honking whistle; kids love just about any toy that makes an antisocial noise! Give a child a drum, a rattle, a whistle, or a trumpet, and they are as happy as can be. This particular trumpet is a real beauty in that it produces a heavy "nose-blowing" honking.

If you like intricate assembly combined with a small amount of hand carving, and if you know of a child with a rude sense of humor and fun, then this project is going to be an all-around winner!

THOUGHTS ON DESIGN AND TECHNIQUE

Once you have thought long and hard on whether you want to favor a lucky child (or disfavor an unlucky parent) with a trumpet that makes a noise that is a cross between a nasty nose-blow and a Daffy Duck call, spend time studying the working drawings (see 12–2). Note that the nose is made as a separate turning. See the way that, once off the lathe, the two-part turning is variously sawn in two, drilled, sliced, worked with a knife and chisel, and reassembled.

Bear in mind that the tricky part is not so much the turning, but rather fitting the mouthpiece "reed." Cutting the blow channel is easy enough, but choosing, cutting, and fitting the reed does require a deal of tenacious and meticulous patience. We experimented with all manner of materials, everything from thin "parchment"-type paper, thick and thin plastic sheet, to a thin shaving of wood and thin plastic film. All of the materials made a noise of sorts. Only thing was that the paper fell apart while the wood became water-logged. In the end, we settled for using the thin plastic sheet because it proved to be the most durable and to make the best noise.

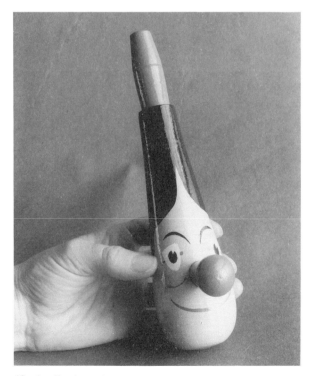

12–1   Project picture.

101

With regard to the shape of the mouthpiece channel and the precise position of the reed, our best advice is to make a mock-up, experiment with various found materials, and take it from there. We made several mouthpieces before we got it right.

Lathe and Tool Considerations

Although we made this project using a chuck, this is not to say that you can't work it between centers.

The only special tools that you need to use are a bench drill press and a ¾-inch-diameter Forstner drill bit. You could, in a pinch, get away with using a brace and an auger bit, but the bench drill press makes the whole procedure that much easier.

Tools and Equipment

Apart from a lathe, you need—
- square-end gouge, parting tool, and skew chisel
- scroll saw
- small knife
- ¼-inch shallow V-section gouge
- bench drill press with two Forstner drill bits—¾ inch and ½ inch
- both a divider and a calliper
- pencil and ruler
- sheet each of tracing and workout paper
- pack of graded sandpapers
- Super Glue
- thin flexible plastic sheet—like photographic film
- two soft-haired watercolor paintbrushes—broad and

fine point
- acrylic paints in the colors black, beige, red, and white
- small quantity of clear varnish
- small roll of double-sided sticky tape

Wood

For this project you need a 12-inch length of easy-to-turn wood three by three inches square for the main body of the trumpet and the mouthpiece, and a small scrap of wood about four-inches long and 1¼ by 1¼ inches square for the nose.

As for the wood type, bear in mind that small children are definitely going to be sucking, blowing, and generally putting the trumpet in their mouths. This being so, it is best to go for a tried-and-tested, lightweight nontoxic wood such as jelutong, sycamore or lime/basswood. Avoid toxic woods such as yew.

TOYMAKING STAGES

Setting Out and First Cuts

Once you have a clear understanding of how the project needs to be worked and put together, and after you have assembled your tools and materials, take the 12-inch length of wood, establish the end center-points by drawing crossed diagonals, and mount it securely on the lathe. Bring up the tool rest, wind up the tailstock, set out your tools, and generally make sure that you and the lathe are in good safe order.

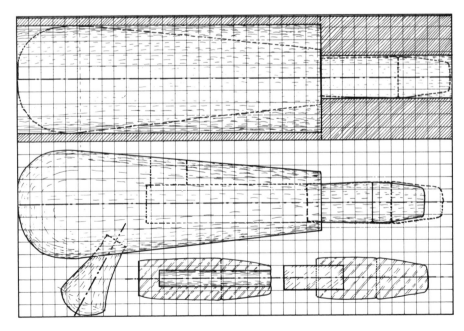

12–2 Working drawings—at a scale of four grid squares to one inch, the finished trumpet measures about nine inches long and 2¼ inches wide.

102

Run through your pre-switch-on checklist, and then switch on the power, take the gouge, and swiftly turn the wood down to the largest possible diameter. Make repeated passes, until you have cleared away the bulk of the waste and the wood is roughly round in section. This done, take the skew chisel, and skim the wood down to a smooth diameter of about 2⅛ inches.

Working from right to left along the cylinder, that is from the tailstock to the chuck, take the divider and set out the initial step-offs (see 12–2, top). Allow about ½ inch for tailstock waste, 2¾ to three inches for the mouthpiece, 6⅜ inches for the body of the trumpet, and the rest for chuck waste. Note that the chuck and tailstock waste aren't shown in the drawing.

Having carefully checked and double-checked that all is correct, take the calliper and the parting tool, and set to work sinking the sizing cuts that define the core diameters. For example, since you are starting out with a cylinder about 2⅛ inches in diameter, and since the mouthpiece needs to finish up at about a ⅞-inch diameter, you need to sink two sizing cuts within the mouthpiece step-off at ⅝ inches.

Sink cuts in to a depth of about ⅜ inch so that you finish up with a larger-than-needed guide diameter of about 1⅜ inches. Lastly, lower the chuck and tailstock waste (see 12–3).

Turning the Profile Curves

With the cylinder cleanly set out with all the step-offs and sizing cuts that make up the design, take the gouge, and swiftly lower the mouthpiece end of the turning to within about ⅛ inch of the required sizing diameter. Next, take the skew chisel, and skim the whole mouthpiece diameter down to ⅞ inch.

When the mouthpiece has been turned down to size, take the divider, and make three step-offs along the total workpiece (see 12–4)—one about 1¼ inches along from the rounded end, one about 1⅛ inches along from the tailstock end, and a final one to mark out the ½-inch length of tailstock waste. Don't cut too deeply, just enough to scratch the surface. Take the skew chisel, and very carefully taper the mouthpiece on either side of the guideline. The mouth end is simple enough; all you need do is turn the taper down to a slightly round-ended diameter of about ⅝ inch. On the other hand, if you have a look at the working drawings (refer to 12–2), you will see that the body end of the mouthpiece is a little more tricky, in that, if it is to be a good wedge-fit in the body hole, it needs to taper to a diameter of ¾ inch. Make successive cuts with the heel of the skew and repeated

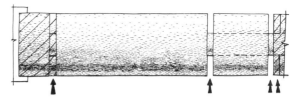

12–3   *Use the parting tool to make sizing cuts at the mouthpiece, and to reduce the tailstock and chuck waste.*

12–4   *Use the divider to set out the primary step-offs.*

12–5   *Lift the handle of the skew chisel until the heel of the blade begins to bite, and then slowly advance the cut to turn down the taper.*

checks with the calliper until the ¾-inch diameter is reached.

When you are ready to turn the body down to size, take the skew chisel, set the bevel flat-down on the guideline, and start by turning the round end to shape. The procedure is much the same as turning a half-ball or a shoulder. You lift the chisel until the heel part begins to bite, and then you take repeated out-and-down cuts. As the half-ball curve begins to take shape, you gradually angle the chisel, so that by the time the heel is sitting in the bottom of the valley, the blade is set vertically with the toe uppermost.

Take the skew chisel, set it flat-down on the other side of the guideline, so that the blade is "looking" towards the tailstock end of the lathe, lift the handle slightly until the heel begins to bite, and then set to work turning down the long taper (see 12–5). The maneuver is beautifully simple; you just make repeated passes from the guideline to the sizing cut at the narrow end of the taper until you reach the required core diameter.

12–6 *Use the toe of the skew chisel to part-off the mouthpiece from the main workpiece.*

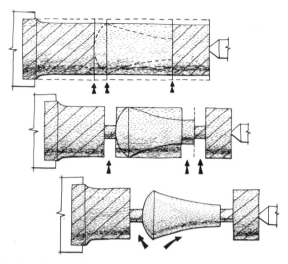

12–7 *(Top) After turning the wood down to a cylinder, mark in the length of the nose and the largest diameter. (Middle) Use the parting tool to clear the waste and to make sizing cuts. (Bottom) Use the skew chisel to model the nose—work from high to low wood.*

Don't try to remove the waste in one great sweep; it is much better to take repeated skims. When you are happy with the shape of the trumpet body, and the mouthpiece, give them a swift rub down with fine-grade sandpaper, part-off the mouthpiece from the lathe (see 12–6), and remove the main part complete with its chuck waste.

Finally, take the small piece of the wood—the bit for the nose—and turn the shape of the nose in the way already described (see 12–7, top to bottom). What we actually did was turn four quite different nose shapes—fat, long, bulbous, and huge—and then chose the one we liked best!

Making the Mouthpiece

Study the working drawings once more (see 12–2, bottom) to see how the mouthpiece needs to be cut, worked, and put together. Take the sausage-shaped turning, and run a pencil guideline down and around its length to divide it in half. Carefully saw it down its length. We used a scroll saw, but you could just as well use a small hand saw, a fret saw, or even split the turning with a knife. Label the two halves, one "top" and the other "bottom."

Take the bottom half, set it down so that the flat face is uppermost, and use a pencil and ruler to mark out the reed trench. The gently sloping trench needs to be open at the mouth end, about ⅜-inch wide, centered down the length of the flat face, and to stop short about ⅜ inch from the trumpet end. Refer to the working drawings (refer to 12–2, bottom). With the guidelines in place, take the penknife and the ¼-dinch wide chisel, and carefully lower the trench so that it slopes from the closed end to about ¼-inch deep at the mouth end. The best procedure is to repeatedly set-in the trench outline with a knife-worked stop-cut, and then, working from the closed end, to skim away the waste with the chisel. With the trench in place, take the top half, and cut ½ inch off the trumpet end. If you now place the two halves together, you will be just about able to see ⅛ inch or so of the closed end of the trench.

Now for the tricky bit! Cut a piece of plastic film about ½-inch wide and 1¼-inches long, and use a tab of double-sided sticky tape to fix it in place on the flat face of the top half so that it sticks out at the cut-off end by about ¾ inch. If you now put the mouthpiece back together, and look down at the cut-off end, the trench should be neatly covered by the plastic reed.

And now for the big test! If you strap the mouthpiece up with a strip of masking tape and give a vigorous blow, the plastic reed should vibrate, making the most awful nose-blowing sound. Fix the two halves together with Super Glue, and put it to one side.

Boring Out the Trumpet

With the trumpet still supported in the chuck, fit the ¾-inch Forstner bit in the drill, and bore a hole straight down into the narrow end of the turning. Aim for a depth of about 3½ inches (see 12–8, left).

Having sawn the trumpet from its piece of waste and sanded it to a good finish, mark in the center points at both ends—at the narrow end and at the round end. Take a strip of masking tape and run it down one side, round the end, up the other side, and across the narrow end so that one side of the tape marks out the centerline. Mark the line with a pencil, and remove the tape (see 12–8, right). Label one side of the trumpet "front" and the other side "back."

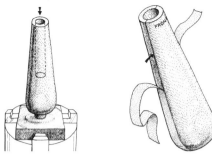

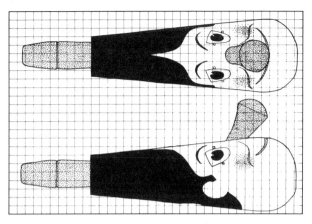

12–8 (Left) With the trumpet still joined to the waste and supported in the chuck, bore a ³⁄₄-inch-diameter hole into the turning to a depth of about 3½ inches. (Right) Having run masking tape around the form to define the midline, mark the line with a pencil, and remove the tape.

12–10 Painting grid—the scale is four grid squares to one inch.

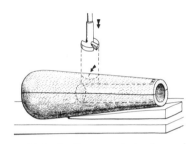

12–9 Bore a ³⁄₄-inch-diameter hole through the back of the trumpet—at the 3¼-inch mark—so that it meets the blind end of the main hole at right angles.

With the main hole bored out, and with a pencil guide mark on the back, set the trumpet shape down so that the "back" side is uppermost, support it on a wedge of scrap—so that the end-to-end axis of the turning is more or less square to the drill bit—and bore a ³⁄₄-inch diameter hole through the back of the trumpet so that it meets the blind end of the main hole at right angles (see 12–9).

Now is a good time to test the noisemaking potential of the trumpet. Blow the sawdust out of the holes, push the mouthpiece in place—and *blow!* If you have got it right, the original nose-blowing noise should be all the more wonderful/awful—depending upon your point of view.

The test complete, fit the ½-inch bit in the drill, and bore out the nose hole at the front. The approach is somewhat the same; the only difference being that the trumpet needs to be angled, wedged, and supported so that the nose can be set at a nice angle to the face. Refer to the working drawings (refer to 12–2, bottom).

PUTTING TOGETHER, FINISHING, AND PAINTING

Start by studying the painting grid (see 12–10), and drawing in the hair line. This done, take your broad paintbrush, and lay on the main areas of ground color; red for the mouthpiece, hat, and nose; black for the hair; and a skin color of your choice for the face. When the ground colors are dry—and you might want to give it a second coat—take the fine-point paintbrush, and articulate all of the little details that make up the face.

TROUBLESHOOTING AND POSSIBLE MODIFICATIONS

• The main difficulties with this project, is cutting the mouthpiece trench and choosing and fitting the reed. Our best advice is to make a prototype, and then experiment with various trench sizes/shapes, and with various reed materials.

· 13 ·

Pull-Along Acrobats

A pull-along toy with two tumbling acrobats; as the wheels go round, the belt-operated figures tumble over and over

Pull-along acrobat toys, as made typically in eighteenth and nineteenth century Germany in the districts of Erzgebirge, Nuremberg, and Berchtesgaden, are truly wonderful playthings. They have all the requirements of a good toy; the imagery is exciting, they are brightly painted, and, best of all, they have movement! Characteristically, the wheels turn a pulley belt, the belt turns a spindle, and the revolving spindle sets little figures tumbling over and over (see 13–1).

It has been said that not only were ingenious toys of this character the prototypes for full-size carts and such, but, more likely than that, it is thought that the eighteenth and nineteenth century craft of toymaking was, as it were, the inspirational forerunner—almost a training ground—for the twentieth century German industries such as optics, car-building, and clock-making.

If you are looking to make a traditional all-wood, pull-along, movement toy—one that involves such woodturning delights as spindle repeats, pivot-jointing, and making balls, beads, and wheels—then this is the project for you! And as for the kids, what child would not

find pleasure in a pull-along toy that features two madcap, strong-men acrobats that tumble and twirl, over and over and over.

THOUGHTS ON DESIGN AND TECHNIQUE

After you have considered the tool, material, and technique implications, of making a toy of this size, type, and complexity, then have a good, long look at the working drawing details (see 13–2).

Note carefully how there is a critical relationship between the length of the figure—the distance between the bottom of the body and the top of the hat—and the length of the arms. That is, if the body is too long or the arms too short, then the tumblers will get stuck and/or the movement might be a good deal less than perfect. And the same goes for the width of the hips in relationship to the spacing of the arms. If you get one or another of the measurements wrong, then it's quite likely that the toy won't work. We're not saying that the project is especially difficult, only that if you don't get the measurements just right, then they are going to be just wrong!

Notice how the main drive spindle is loosely pivoted between the two pillars with a tight glue-fix through the arms, while the limbs are loosely pivoted at both the hips and shoulders. Evaluate the way that the wheels turn the pulley belt, the belt turns the main spindle, and the spindle raises and lowers the figures—all with the effect that the figures flip over on their loose-fit shoulder pivots.

Finally, when you know what goes where and how, be mindful that the success of the project hinges—perhaps more so with this project than some of the others—on you being a fairly confident turner.

Lathe and Tool Considerations

Although this project has to do with turning repeats—two pillars, two bodies, four legs, and so on—since the

13–1 Project picture.

components are small, you can do quite well using only a basic "starter" lathe. As to whether you need to use a chuck to hold the wood, you can, if you so wish, turn all of the components between centers—even the wheels. We chose to turn the wheels with the wood held in a four-jaw chuck—its wonderfully easy and direct—but you could just as well use a screw chuck or even a small homemade wooden chuck.

Tools and Equipment

Apart from a lathe, you need—
- gouge—square or round nosed
- parting tool and skew chisel
- drill bits in the sizes ⅛, 3/16, ¼, ⅜, ½, and ¾ inch. We use Forstner bits for the larger sizes
- bench drill press
- small-toothed gents saw
- both dividers and callipers
- pencil and ruler
- sheet each of tracing and workout paper
- length of brass picture wire with a toggle at each end—for making decorative friction burns
- pack of graded sandpapers
- two soft-haired watercolor paintbrushes—broad and fine point
- acrylic paints in the colors yellow, green, black, and red
- small quantity of clear, high-gloss varnish
- two 1½-inch long roundhead brass screws for the wheels, and four ¾-inch long roundhead brass screws for the leg pivots
- Super Glue

Wood

We used beech for the figures, pillars, base, and dowels, and jelutong for the wheels. You will need—
- 20-inch length of 1¼ by 1¼ inch square section wood for the two pillars
- nine-inch length of 1½ by 1½ inch section wood for the two bodies
- six-inch length of 1¼ by 1¼ inch section wood for the two double-arms
- 10-inch length of 1¼ by 1¼ inch section wood for the five bead-balls
- 12-inch length of one by one inch section wood for the four legs
- six-inch length of three by three inch section wood for the three wheels
- eight-inch length of prepared one by two inch section wood for the base
- selection of dowels for the various pivots and shafts

TOYMAKING STAGES

Turning the Pillars

When you have gathered together all your tools and materials, and when you have variously made full-size drawings and tracings, pencil-label all your lengths of wood, and get organized for turning.

Take the 20-inch length of 1¼ by 1¼ inch square section wood—the piece for the pillars—establish the position of the end centers by drawing crossed diagonals, and mount it on the lathe. Bring the tool rest up to the workpiece, turn the wood over by hand, just to make sure it is unobstructed, and then switch on the power. Use the gouge to swiftly turn the wood down to the largest possible round section. This done, use the calliper and the skew chisel to further turn the wood down to a smooth 1⅛-inch diameter.

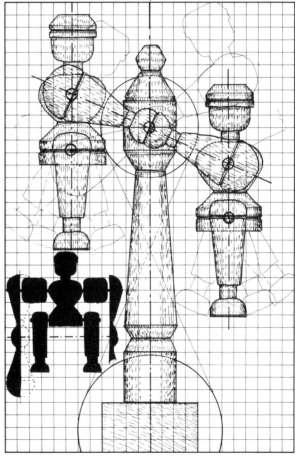

13–2 *Working drawings—at a scale of two grid squares to one inch, the finished toy stands about 12 inches high, and is almost 10 inches wide across the span of the wheels.*

107

Take the ruler and divider, and, starting at the head-stock, set out all of the step-offs that go to make up the design. After allowing for a small amount of chuck waste, the step-off sequence should be one inch for the spigot, one inch for the bottom of the pillar, two step-offs of $5/16$ inch for the decorative waist or V-cut, three inches for the long taper, $1/2$ inch for the shoulder, two $1/2$-inch step-offs for the main bead, $1/2$ inch for the top shoulder, and a last $1/2$ inch for the top finial (see 13–3, left). When you get this far, allow $1/4$ inch for between-pillar waste, and then reverse and repeat the step-offs for the twin pillar.

With the step-offs clearly set out, use the parting tool and the skew chisel to cut-in, or size, the primary diameters. The spigot is easy enough; all you do is run the parting tool into the required depth, and then clear the waste. The taper and the angled shoulders are a little

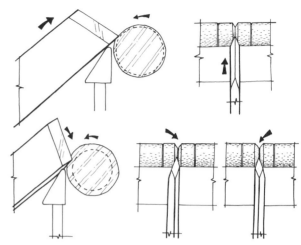

13–4 (Top) Hold the skew chisel so that the toe is pointing downwards, and set the guideline in with a shallow V-cut. (Bottom) Hold the skew chisel so that the toe is uppermost, and angle it from side to side to deepen the V-cut.

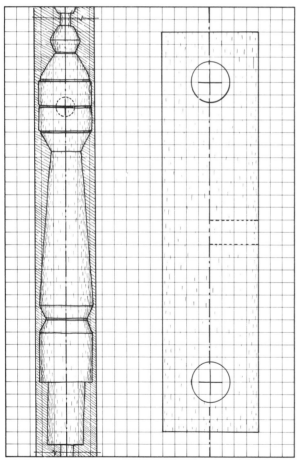

13–3 Working drawings—the scale is four grid squares to one inch. (Left) The pillar profile. (Right) Plan of the base—note the position of the pillar spigot holes and the pull-dowel hole.

more difficult. What we usually do is take the skew chisel, turn it over so that the toe is pointing downwards (see 13–4, top), and then set to work cutting in the depth guides. The procedure is much the same as when you are using the parting tool to set the depth guides; the only real difference is that the bottom of the guide is more of a V-cut than a square trench.

Set the line in with the toe of the skew, then turn the chisel over and cut the score line a little deeper . . . and so on (see 13–4, bottom). The idea is that when you size with a skew chisel, it is the bottom of the V-cut that marks out the required diameter. And the other point to bear in mind is that when you are turning the taper, or whatever, you might have to achieve your diameter with several little-by-little passes rather than a single thrust. For example, with the long taper the best procedure is to make a V-cut at the top of the taper—where it meets the angled shoulder—then run the skew chisel along the wood to begin the taper. When you have made the first downhill cut or bite, use the calliper to assess the situation, and then make successive guide cuts and bites until the required taper and diameter is achieved. Continue cutting the decorative V-cut around the base of the pillar, cutting the angled shoulders, and so on, all the way to the top finial.

Once you have used the skew chisel to bring the turnings to a final smooth finish, take the brass wire, and embellish the steps and V-cuts with decorative friction-burnt bands.

Turning the Arms

Analyze the working drawings once again (see 13–5, top), and see how the arms are all worked from a single turning. Take the six-inch length of 1¼ by 1¼ inch section wood, fix the end center points, and mount it securely on the lathe. Swiftly turn the wood down to a diameter of about 1⅛ inch.

With the wood turned to a cylinder, mark in a half-way point three inches along from one end. With the ruler and divider, work out from the halfway mark setting out all of the step-offs that make up the design. From end to end, the sequence is a small amount for chuck waste, ½ inch for the broad half-ball end, 1¼ inches for the taper, ¼ inch for the wrist, and ½ inch for the half-boss. When you reach the center-point, then reverse and repeat the measurements for the other end of the turning.

Set the calliper to about ⅜ inch, and then take the parting tool, and turn the wrist down to size. The procedure is very straightforward; all you do is start the wrist step-off with the parting tool, set the calliper on the wrist, and then continue lowering the waste until the calliper slips over the wood. Cut a wrist on each side of the central boss. While the tools are at hand, reduce the boss area to a diameter of ¾ inch. With the necks cut and all the primary guidelines in place, take the skew chisel, and turn the tapers. One taper at a time, use the toe of the skew chisel to make a single guide or sizing cut— halfway along the taper—and then use the heel of the skew to make progressive downhill passes (see 13–6). Continue until the taper runs in a smooth, straight line from the shoulder-pivot line to the wrist.

Having turned both tapers, then comes a favorite bit, which is turning the round shoulders or beads. The technique is beautifully simple; all you do is take the skew chisel, lay the bevel on the high point, roll the tool over until it begins to bite at the heel, and then roll the chisel down-and-round to cut the downhill curve. Make repeated passes until you achieve the desired form. Repeat this procedure to turn the round half-ball ends and the central boss. Finally, after using the skew chisel to skim the turning down to a smooth finish, friction-burn the decorative lines, and part-off the turning from the lathe.

Turning the Figure and the Beads

Refresh your eye and have another look at the working drawings (see 13–5, middle). Take the nine-inch length of 1½ by 1½ inch section wood, and mount it securely on the lathe, as already described. Use the gouge and the

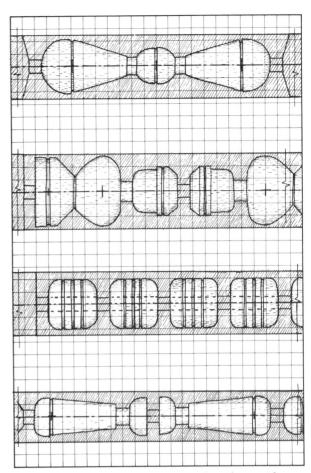

13–5 Working drawings—the scale is four grid squares to one inch. (Top) Arms. (Middle) Body and beads. (Bottom) Legs.

13–6 Turn the taper by using the heel of the skew to make progressive downhill passes.

skew chisel to turn the wood down to a smooth 1⅜-inch diameter cylinder. This done, take the ruler and divider, and set out all of the step-offs that make up the design. With the two figures arranged so that they are head to head, and working from left to right along the work-piece, the step-off sequence is a small amount for head-stock waste, ½ inch for the base, ½ inch for the hips, ½ inch up to the chest line, ½ inch for the shoulders, ¼ inch for the neck, ½ inch for the face, ³⁄₁₆ inch for the hat brim, and ¼ inch for the top of the hat. When you reach this point, allow ¼-inch for waste, and then reverse and repeat the step-offs for the other figure.

Use the calliper and parting tool to turn selected step-offs down to a smaller diameter. The neck needs to be about ⅜ inch, the face ¾ inch, and the brim of the hat at more or less than one inch. When you have "stepped" the figure, then take the skew chisel—as already described—and cut the various tapers, angles, and curves. Once again, if you want to go for a more fancy profile, have more decorative V-cuts, or whatever, then this is the time to go your own way. Finally, skim the turning to a good finish, give it a swift rub down with fine-grade sandpaper, burn in the decorative lines, and part-off from the lathe.

When you come to turning the five beads—meaning the large balls that go between the body and the arms and at the end of the spindle—all you do is mount the 10-inch length of 1¼ by 1¼ inch section wood in the way already described, set out the step-offs in the sequence—headstock waste and one inch for each of the balls, with ¼-inch step-offs of waste in between—and then follow the procedure for turning beads and round shoulders, and for burning lines, as already described.

Turning the Legs

Turning the legs is much the same procedure as already described—refer to the working drawings (see 13–5, bottom). That is, the wood is mounted between centers, marked out with the divider, reduced in diameter at selected step-offs, and then further worked with the skew chisel. The difficulty is not so much in the individual procedures—they are straightforward enough—the difficulty is in achieving a well-matched group of four near-identical turnings. The best way is to set out pairs of legs together—foot to foot—and then to work all four legs all-of-a-piece. So you might work all the hip curves, and then all the tapers, and so on, along the string of turnings.

Finally, when you have what you consider are four well-matched legs, skim them to a good finish, and part them off one at a time from the lathe.

Turning the Wheels

Take your six-inch length of three by three inch square section wood—we used jelutong for no other reason than we didn't have beech of the correct size—establish

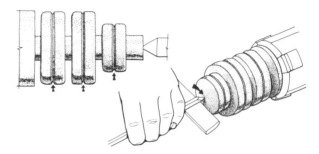

13–7 (Top) Aim for a V-cut at about ⅛-inch deep and ⅛-inch wide. (Bottom) Mark in the center-point and part-off.

the end centers by drawing crossed diagonals, and mount it securely on the lathe. Grip it firmly in your chosen chuck.

Take the large gouge, and swiftly turn the wood down to the largest possible diameter. This done, take the divider, and, working from right to left along the workpiece—that is, from the tailstock center back towards the headstock—set out the step-offs in the sequence one inch for waste, one inch for the small wheel, ¼ inch for waste, one inch for one rolling wheel, ¼ inch for waste, one inch for the other rolling wheel, and the remainder for tailstock waste.

Take the parting tool, and sink the bands of waste to a depth of one inch so that you are left with a core at about one inch in diameter. Next, reduce the first wheel in line—the one nearest the tailstock—down to a diameter of about two inches. Having used the skew chisel to skim each wheel to a smooth finish and to turn off the sharp edges, use the toe of the skew to cut the V-slot. Bearing in mind, that on two of the wheels the slot is functional, aim for a V-cut that is about ⅛-inch wide and ⅛-inch deep (see 13–7, top).

Once you are satisfied with the overall shape and finish of the three wheels, wind the tailstock back out of the way, set the tool rest up over the bed of the lathe so that you can approach the wood end-on, and use the parting tool and the skew chisel to turn the face of the first wheel in line down to a good finish. Be sure to mark a clear center-point (see 13–7, bottom). Having faced the first wheel, reposition the tool rest so that you can approach the wood side-on, and then carefully part-off the finished wheel.

SAWING, DRILLING AND SANDING

Start by using the small saw to cut the arm turning down into two flat-faced units. The procedure is a little bit tricky, so take your time. The easiest method—after first drawing a pencil line that runs from end to end around the turning—is to support it in a long V-block, and to then saw down through the long face (see 13–8, top). We've tried using the scroll saw and such, but using the hand saw is easier in the long run.

When you have achieved two near identical flat-faced half-turnings—like two bowtie shapes—rub them down on a sheet of sandpaper until the flat faces are smooth and true. While the sandpaper is at hand, take the four legs, reduce the wood with a craft knife (see 13–8, bottom), and rub them down to leave opposite sides with a flat face that runs from the hip end down to the ankle.

When you have sorted out the arms and legs, then comes the not-so-easy task of drilling all the holes. They have to be right; so spend time measuring and double-checking. The wheels are straightforward enough; all you do is bore ¼-inch holes through all the centers—and the same goes for the beads.

Drill Sizes

- For the figures—bore a ¼-inch hole that runs from side to side through the line of the shoulders.
- For the arms—run three ¼-inch holes through each double-arm unit, one hole through the center of the boss, and one hole through each of the two shoulder lines.
- For the legs—bore a single ⅛-inch hole through the flat face and in line with the burnt groove.
- For the pillars—bore a single ⅜-inch hole through the top of the pillar and in line with the middle decorative groove. Make sure that both pillars are as nearly as possible identical.
- For the base holes (see 13–3, right)—draw a center line that runs from end to end down the length of the two-inch wide face, measure in one inch along from the ends, and then bore a ¾-inch diameter hole through the one-inch thickness. Next, having fixed the center-point by drawing diagonals across the eight inch by one inch face, bore a ½-inch-wide hole to a depth of about 1 inch. Have a trial assembly (see 13–9).

PAINTING AND PUTTING TOGETHER

We have gone for green wheels, a yellow drive spindle wheel, yellow suits, and green hats. Lay on a couple of coats for good coverage, and put them to one side to dry.

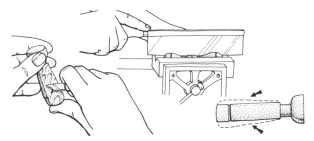

13–8 (Top) Support the arms in a long V-block, and use a gents saw to cut through the long face. (Bottom) Reduce the sides of the legs with a craft knife, and sand the cut faces to a smooth finish.

13–9 Have a trial assembly prior to painting.

Next, use the fine-point paintbrush to articulate the small details on the face—black eyes and a red nose, mouth, and costume.

When the paint is dry, start assembly by setting the pillars in their holes and screwing on the rolling wheels. After drilling pilot holes for the screws, screw the legs in place on the sides of the figures. Next, slide the ¼-inch-diameter drive spindle dowel in place so that it runs through the top-of-the-pillar holes, through the arms, and on through the small drive wheel and the spindle bead. With the spindle and arms in position, set the body and beads in place between the arms, and slide a thinner dowel through the whole works. Do this for both figures. Lastly, set the ½-inch diameter pull-dowel in the side of the base, fit an elastic band around the rolling and drive wheel grooves, and have a trial run.

Once you are happy with the movement—and this will take some time to get right—use Super Glue to fix the pillar spigots in the base, the drive wheel and ball on the ends of the spindle, the arms on the spindle, and the pull-dowel in the base.

· 14 ·

Rocking Horse and Rider

A small turned and carved tabletop rocking horse with a soldier rider

The horse is, without a doubt, one of the most popular toy forms of all time. From the woodturner's viewpoint, one of the most interesting types is the small "dish" rocker (see 14–1) as made in the eighteenth and nineteenth centuries in the mountains between Germany and Czechoslovakia—in the region known as Erz or Erzgebirge by the Germans, and Krusne Hory by the Czechs.

We must not forget the kids! They will really enjoy the principal feature that the wedge-fit rider can be removed and played with as a separate toy.

THOUGHTS ON DESIGN AND TECHNIQUE

After you have considered the tool, material, and technique ramifications of building a toy of this size, type and complexity, then have a good, long look at the details of the working drawings (see 14–2). See how we have modified the traditional design and way of working by having the rocker base made from a single dish that has been cut in half and then reassembled (see 14–3). Notice that we have made another modification by making the

horse's head and the backrest from another turning (see 14–4). That said, if you want to make a whole run of identical horses, then you could change the design some-

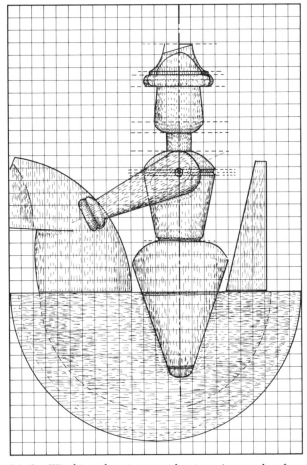

14–2   Working drawings—side view. At a scale of four grid squares to one inch, the finished toy stands about eight inches high, and almost seven inches long from nose to tail.

14–1   Project picture.

112

what so that you get two rocker bases from a single turning, four heads from another, and so on.

Consider how the head turning is first sliced in half and then reassembled and quartered before being further sliced and worked. Once again, if you want to turn out a large output all at once, you could change the design slightly so that a single disc or pill shape gives you four horses' heads.

Have a look at the painting grid (see 14–11), and see how the turning that goes to make the rider needs to be sanded at front and back and cut away so that it can fit astride the rocker. The fun of this project is playing around with the turnings and working out more efficient ways of putting the horse together.

Lathe and Tool Considerations

Of all the projects in the book, this one is unusual in that it requires the use of a pretty full range of lathe accessories. You need a small screw chuck, a six-inch faceplate, a four-jaw chuck, and a sanding disc. You could do without the screw chuck, and, perhaps, you could work the soldier between centers rather than have it held in the four-jaw chuck, but the sanding disc is a must. We say this, because a great deal of the shaping—of the horse's head and the soldier—is done by "stroke carving" the wood along the edge of the sanding disc. As to sawing the various turnings, although we use both a small band saw and a coping saw, this is not to say that you can't make-do with just a coping saw, or even with a tenon saw, a chisel, and rasp.

Tools and Equipment

Apart from a lathe, you need—
- six-inch faceplate and small screw chuck
- sanding disc to fit on the bowl-turning end of the lathe
- square-end gouge, skew chisel, and parting tool
- round-nosed gouge and round-nosed scraper
- small band saw and coping saw
- single, ⅛-inch diameter drill bit, bench drill press
- dividers, callipers, pencil, and ruler
- sheet each of tracing and workout paper
- two small, ⅛-inch-diameter roundhead brass screws for the arm pivots
- graded sandpapers
- two soft-haired watercolor paintbrushes—broad and fine point
- acrylic paints in the colors green, black, white, blue, beige-pink, red, and gold
- small quantity of clear high-gloss varnish
- Super Glue

Wood

For this project you need—
- 2½-inch-thick slab of jelutong about 6½ by 6½ inches square—for the dish that makes the rocker base
- one-inch-thick slab of jelutong six by six inches square—for the disc that makes the horse's head and the backrest
- 12-inch length of jelutong three by three inches square—for the soldier

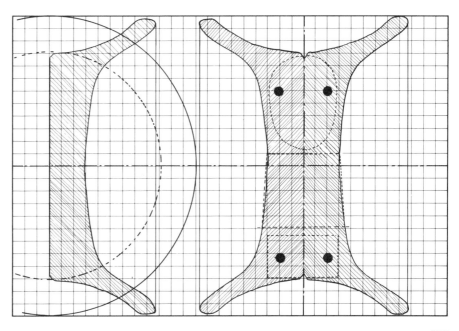

14–3 Working drawings— plan and section view of the horse rocker dish. The scale is four grid squares to one inch. Note the position of the fixing pegs.

113

Turning the Rocker Base

Carefully study the project picture (see 14–1) and the working drawings (see 14–3). Take the 2½-inch-thick slab of 6½ by 6½ inch square wood—the piece of birch for the rocker base—fix a center point by drawing crossed diagonals on one square face, and slice away the bulk of the corner waste on the band saw. Now, using the shortest possible screws, screw holes that are positioned about 1½ inches in from the edge of the plate, screw the wood securely to the faceplate. Screw the whole works on the headstock spindle, bring the tool rest up so that you can approach it edge-on, check that you and the lathe are in good safe order, and switch on the power.

Take your gouge—we used the round-nosed—and very carefully turn away the irregular edges of the wood.

14–5 Hollow out the bowl so that you are left with a base thickness of about ¾ inch. Mark in the center point.

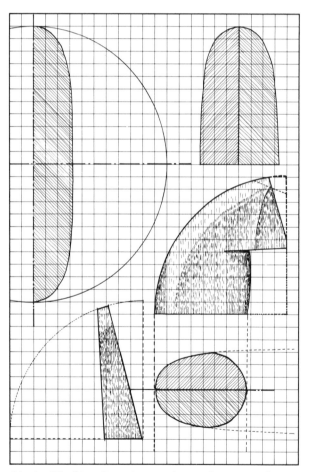

14–4 Working Drawings—plan and sections showing how the "mushroom" turning is sandwiched and quartered to make the head and the seat rest. The scale is four grid squares to one inch.

Continue until you have the largest possible disc. This done, reposition the tool rest over the bed of the lathe so that you can approach the disc face-on. Still working with the gouge, turn the face down to a smooth finish. Keep marking the center point with a pencil.

Having turned the basic disc, put the tool rest back so that you can work the wood edge-on. Now, take the parting tool, and run a single guide cut alongside the face of the plate and into the wood to a depth of about ¼ inch. With the depth-cut in place, take the tool of your choice, and set to work turning the concave edge-of-dish profile. Aim to run a smooth curve from right to left into the wood—that is, from the rim of the bowl to the base.

Once you have achieved the outer profile of the bowl, move the tool rest back over the bed of the lathe so that you can approach the disc of wood face-on. Working first with the round-nosed gouge and then the scraper, hollow out the bowl so that you are left with a base thickness of about ¾ inch (see 14–5). When you are happy with the overall form, rub the whole bowl down with a piece of fine-grade sandpaper, and take it off the lathe.

Turning the Pill for the Horse's Head and the Seat Rest

Take the one-inch thick, six by six inch slab of jelutong, repeat the prelathe procedures as already described. Aim for a total diameter of about 5½ inches and a thickness of a little over ¾ inch. Refer to the working drawings (see 14–4).

Position the tool rest over the lathe bed so that you can work the wood face-on. Now, working in the direction of the grain—that is from the center out towards the side—turn down the sharp edge to create a convex profile that runs in a smooth curve from the center of the disc to the back side-edge.

114

Finally, when you have roughed out the form with the gouge, and skimmed it off to a good finish with the skew chisel, rub it down with fine-grade sandpaper, and remove it from the lathe.

Turning the Soldier Rider

Carefully study the working drawings. Take the 12-inch length of three by three inch square-section of jelutong, establish the end centers by drawing crossed diagonals, and mount it securely on the lathe. Start by taking the gouge and the skew chisel, and turning it down to a smooth round section 2½ inches in diameter. This done, take the divider and, working from right to left along the cylinder, set-out the step-offs—½ inch for tailstock waste, 1⅝ inches for the rider's legs, one inch for the hips, 1⅜ inches for the tapered lower body, ⅜ inch for the rounded shoulders, ⅜ inch for the neck, ⅞ inch for the head, ¼ inch for the hat brim, ⅝ inch for the crown of the hat, ¼ inch for waste, and the remainder for the hand-arm and chuck waste. Don't attempt to start the arm at this stage. When you have double-checked that all the step-off spacings are correct, then use the gouge, the skew chisel, the parting tool, and the calliper to turn down all the waste—as described in the other projects. From right to left along the workpiece, the step-off diameters should run 2½ inches for the legs and hips, 1½ inches for the taper and shoulders, ½ inch for the neck, one inch for the head, 1⅜ inches for the hat brim, 1¼ inches for the crown of the hat, and ½ inch for the waste between the hat and the hand-end of the arm (see 14–6).

When you are happy with the basic turning, and when you have checked with the callipers, take the skew chisel, and use the toe to make V-cuts at the foot, hip, and shoulder lines. Run the cuts to a depth of about 1/16 inch.

With all the ground work complete, take the skew chisel, and set to work on all the tapers and curves that make up the design.

Starting with the leg section, and working with the skew chisel, the cutting procedure is to set the bevel flat-down on the hip line—so that the cutting edge is "looking" towards the tailstock—gradually to ease the handle upwards until the cutting edge begins to bite, and then smoothly to advance, making the cut. Run the gentle taper down to the foot line, deepen the line slightly, and then roundover the bottom edge to make a curved foot that runs into the base.

When you come to turning the large curved bead or round shoulder that goes to make the hips, all you do is repeat the procedure and work in the other direction. If all is well, the heel will finish up sitting in the valley at the bottom of the waist line. Be wary of being too heavy-

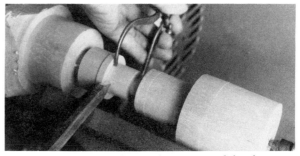

14–6　*Turn the wood to a clean, stepped finish.*

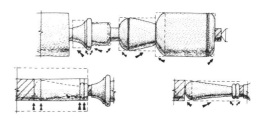

14–7　*(Top) Use the skew chisel and, working from high to low wood, slowly turn the stepped form down to the curved profile. (Bottom left) Turn the whole arm down to a cylinder of about ⅞ inch, and mark in all the step-offs. (Bottom right) Turn the curve of the shoulders, the arm taper, and the side-by-side beads that form the two hands.*

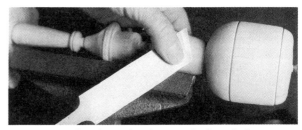

14–8　*Use the skew chisel to work the whole turning to a super-smooth finish. Support the workpiece, while at the same time applying pressure with your thumb. Aim for a feather-light stroke.*

handed—it is much better to settle for making a series of small repeat cuts until you have what you consider is a good form. Continue with all the other forms that go to make up the design (see 14–7).

With the body more or less finished, reduce the diameter of the section of wood between the hat and the chuck, and get busy making the arm and hand.

Turn the whole arm down to a cylinder about ⅞ inches in diameter, mark in all the step-offs with the dividers (see 14–7, bottom left), reduce the diameter even further, and then turn the curve of the shoulder, the taper of the arm, and the two side-by-side beads that make the ball of the hand.

As the workpiece gets closer to completion, take the skew chisel, and skim the whole works to a good finish (see 14–8). Use the toe of the skew chisel to redefine the V-cuts at the hips, shoulders, and hands. Give the whole turning a swift rub down with fine-grade sandpaper.

Once you have achieved a cleanly turned form, take the parting tool, and, starting at the tailstock end, tidy-up the foot and part-off the waste, and part-off the figure from the hand-arm. When you come to cut through the small amount of waste, try to leave the hat and the end of the hand in good order. The best procedure is to support the figure in one hand and part-off with the other. Finally, tidy-up the round end of the arm, and part-off the arm from the chuck waste.

Putting the Horse Together

Take the six-inch diameter dish, set it rim-side down on the worksurface, and establish the diameter by running a strip of masking tape through the center point. Have the dividing line aligned so that it runs in the direction of the grain. Run the dish through the band saw to cut it in half. Take the two half-dishes, dribble a generous amount of Super Glue over what was the bottom of the dish—over both mating halves—and then set the halves base to base to make the rocker. Spend time making sure that the dish rims are nicely aligned. When the glue is dry, sand the top of the rocker—meaning the sawn face—to a completely smooth, level finish.

Take the pill disc, and repeat the cutting, gluing, and sanding procedure, as already described. Make sure that the rounded curve edges, at what will be the back of the horse's neck, are carefully aligned.

If you now look at the working drawings (refer to 14–4), you will see that the horse's head comes from one two-quarter sandwich, and the backrest from the other. Pencil-label the head sandwich, and arrange it so that the grain runs vertically from the base line to the top of the mane. This done, trace the head design from the working drawings, and press-transfer the image to the wood. Adjust the flat drawing to fit the curved surface of the wood, hatch in the areas that need to be cut away, and generally make sure that you know what goes where and how. If all is well, the "neck"—meaning the face of the wood that sits on top of the rocker—should measure no more than 1⅞ inches along the join line.

With all the guidelines in place, use the band saw to swiftly cut away the two bits of waste—the small trian-

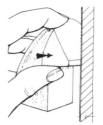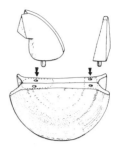

14–9 (Left) Use the disc sander to angle the checks down to the nose. (Right) Drill and peg-dowel the head and the seat rest to the top of the rocker.

gle from above the nose, and the rectangle from under the jaw. This done, move to the disc sander, and set to work shaping the head. The face is easy enough; all you do is sand the sawn edge flat and angle the cheeks down towards the nose (see 14–9, left). And the same goes for the ears; all you do is use the edge of the disc to sand a little V-groove on the top of the head.

When you come to shaping the front of the neck, roll the wood along the edge of the sanding disc to rub down the sharp edges, and to give the neck an oval- or egg-shaped section at its base. Refer to the working drawings (see 14–4, bottom right). Shape the curve around the front of the neck so that the flat underside of the jaw runs in a straight line to each side of the head. The seat rest is wonderfully easy; all you do is first make two straight passes on the band saw to cut away the large areas of waste, and then sand the sawn faces to a smooth finish.

Sand and fit the head and the backrest in position on the rocker so that there is the biggest possible space for the soldier rider, and pencil-mark the placing. Allow about 1⅞ inches between the back of the head and the front of the backrest. Finally, drill and peg-dowel the head and the backrest to the top of the rocker so that each has two dowels (see 14–3)—and dry-fit (see 14–9).

Making and Fitting the Soldier

Before you do anything else, have a look again at the project picture (see 14–1), and the working drawings (see 14–4), and see how all of the flat faces, apart from underneath the legs, are achieved on the sanding disc.

Put in as many guidelines and shadings as you need. With all the lines in place, start by sanding away the sides and top of the hat. Sand the sides of the hat so that the side brims are just a fraction wider than the side of the face. The shoulders are delightfully easy; a quick touch to the sander of each side of the shoulder, and the job is done.

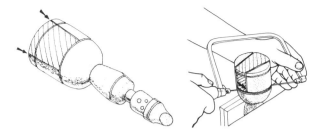

14–10   (Left) Make two straight cuts with the band saw to define the width and depth of the waste. (Right) Slice away the waste with the coping saw.

Having sanded the hat and shoulders, then comes the tricky task of cutting away the between-leg waste, and shaping the flat areas at the front and back of the legs. We say tricky, because although the guidelines are a help, most of the work has to be done by eye. Start by sitting the turning in place on top of the horse, and drawing the curved "saddle" shape on the bottom of the turning (see 14–3, right). This done, use the band saw and the coping saw to chop out the waste. The best procedure is to make two straight cuts with the band saw (see 14–10, left)—to define the width and depth of the waste—and then to complete the operation with the coping saw (see 14–10, right). Make two band-saw cuts into the turning up as far as the hip or saddle line, and then link the two cuts so that the chunk of waste falls away.

When you have chopped out the waste, go back to the sander and sand the figure at front and back so that, when seen in side view, the legs angle in a straight line from the top of the hips to the feet. The legs should be about 1½ inches wide at the saddle line and the feet should be about ½ inch or so at the bottom. Continue sanding, trimming, and generally easing until the figure sits fair and square on the horse.

Take the single arm turning, and saw it from hand to shoulder down the middle so that you have two corresponding flat-faced "split" turnings. As needed, sand the sawn faces to a smooth finish. This done, set the arms on either side of the body, mark the screw holes, and bore them with a ⅛-inch drill bit. Sand the outer curves of the arm flat at the holes so that the screw heads fit flush, and screw them in place on the side of the body.

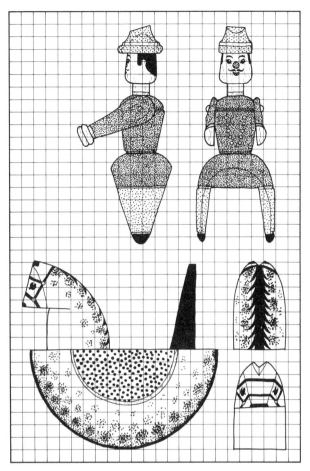

14–11   Painting grid—the scale is about three grid squares to one inch.

PAINTING AND FINISHING

Start by painting in the main areas of ground color. When you come to applying the dappled areas, take the broad paintbrush, dip it into an almost-dry dollop of black paint, and dry-brush, or "print," the horse with a dabbing action. Use the fine-point paintbrush to paint in the details.

Once the acrylic paint is completely dry, give the whole works a couple of coats of clear varnish. Finally, screw the arms in place, glue and peg the horse's head and backrest, and trim the soldier's hat with braid and a feather. The toy is finished and the fun can begin.

117

· 15 ·

Farm Tractor and Trailer

A push–pull tractor with steerable front wheels and a hitching peg with a link-up bar to the steerable flatbed trailer including six removable load poles and a delivery of logs

Most kids, and quite a few adults, enjoy nothing better than crawling around on the floor playing with push–pull toys—cars, trucks, trains, and planes.

If you have mastered the art and craft of woodturning, and if you know of kids who like push–pull carpet vehicles—sons, daughters, grandchildren, nephews, nieces, or just the children next door—then you are going to have a great time with this project (see 15–1). If you want to make a really beautiful, hardy traditional toy—the type of toy that might have been around in the 1940s and 50s—a toy that will last several generations, then this project will give you many hours of woodturning pleasure.

THOUGHTS ON DESIGN AND TECHNIQUE

After you have considered the tool, material, and technique implications of building a toy of this complexity—it is a large toy of many parts and requires a high skill level and a full range of tools—then spend a good, long time studying all the working drawings and details.

15–1 Project picture.

Of all the parts that make up this toy, we are most pleased with the guards that go over the large tractor wheels. If you look at the working drawings (see 15–2), you will see that the two, identical guards have been made from a single dish turning that has been sawn in half and then sanded to shape. Note also the way that the steering rod with its axle block has been turned with two steps, or spigots, along its length, drilled, and shaped.

Start by drawing all the working drawings to full size.

Lathe and Tool Considerations

For this project you need a screw chuck, a woodgripping chuck—we use, as always, a four-jaw chuck—a sanding disc on the bowl-turning end of the lathe, plus the usual range of turning tools. You also need a bench drill press with a good range of Forstner drill bits.

Tools and Equipment

Apart from a lathe, you need—
- small screw chuck
- sanding disc to fit on the bowl-turning end of the lathe
- square-end gouge and round-nosed gouge
- parting tool and skew chisel
- round-nosed scraper
- small band saw and coping saw
- bench drill press with a good range of Forstner bits
- dividers and callipers, pencil and ruler
- sheet each of tracing and workout paper
- good assortment of roundhead brass screws with washers to fit
- pack of graded sandpapers
- two soft-haired, watercolor, paintbrushes—broad and fine point
- acrylic paints in the colors green, black, white, and red

- quantity of clear high-gloss varnish
- 12-inch length of stainless steel/aluminum coat-hanger-type wire for the trailer link-up arm
- Super Glue

Wood

We used jelutong throughout this project. You will need—

- one-inch thick slab of prepared wood 2½ inches wide and nine inches long—for the tractor chassis
- one-inch slab of prepared wood five inches wide and seven inches long—for the trailer bed
- 10-inch length of three by three inch square section wood—for the tractor engine block/hood and the two front wheels
- 15-inch length of three by three inch square section wood—for the four trailer wheels, the two trailer axle blocks, and the bucket seat
- nine-inch length of 1½ by 1½ inch square section wood—for the tractors, the steering rod and axle block
- two one-inch-thick slabs of wood 5½ by 5½ inches square—for the two large tractor wheels
- 1¼-inch slab of wood 6½ by 6½ inches square—for the two wheel guards
- good selection of workshop off-cuts—for all the other bits and pieces
- 60-inch length of ½-inch-diameter, shop-bought wooden dowel—for the various axle rods and posts

TOYMAKING STAGES

Turning the Engine Block and the Two Front Tractor Wheels

Start by having a good long look at the working drawings (see 15–2). Take the 10-inch length of three by three inch square-section wood, and check it over just to make sure that it is free from splits, stains, and all the other faults that might well hinder your progress. Establish the end center point by drawing crossed diagonals, and mount it securely on the lathe—in the chuck and pivoted on the tailstock center. Bring up the tool rest, and make sure that all your tools are comfortably at hand. Use the gouge and the skew chisel to turn the wood down to a smooth diameter cylinder that is as near as possible to three inches. As usual, the procedure is to remove the corners of waste with the gouge, and then to tidy-up with the skew chisel.

Having turned the wood down to the basic cylinder, take the divider and set out all of the step-offs that make

up the design. Working from right to left along the wood allow ½ inch for the tailstock waste and the engine button/detail, 4½ inches for the engine, ¼ inch for parting-off waste, 1½ inches for the first wheel, ¼ inch for parting-off waste, 1½ inches for the second wheel, ¼ inch for parting-off waste, and the remainder for chuck waste. Still using the divider, and still working from right to left along the wood, mark out the engine block with a step-off at one inch for the round end, and five step-offs at about ½ inch and one at ¾ inch for the last decorative groove. Don't worry too much if the grooves vary in size; they are only decorative. Divide each of the two wheels into three equal ½-inch-wide step-offs.

With all the step-off guide marks in place, take the parting tool, and start by sinking all the bands of waste to a depth of one inch—so that you are left with a central

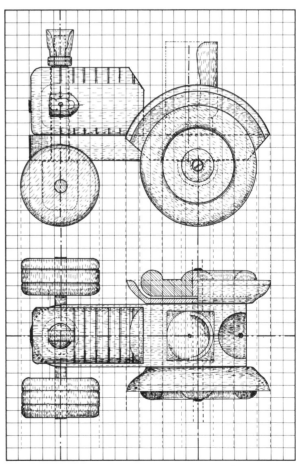

15–2 Working drawings—the tractor, side view and plan. At a scale of two grid squares to one inch, the finished tractor stands about eight inches high, 10 inches long, and six inches wide across the span of the front wheels.

core at about one inch. You should be left with three clean-cut cylinders, the engine block/body and two wheels all marked out with guidelines and ready to go. If all is correct, take the skew chisel, and use the toe to cut the decorative V-grooves at each end of the engine cylinder. The procedure is to push the toe in, to fix the depth of the groove, and then either to withdraw the chisel and enter the toe in from each side of the cut, or to turn the chisel over, lay the bevel on the high wood to the side of the cut, and slice down with the heel.

Starting at the tailstock end of the engine cylinder, set the blade flat-down on the high spot to the right of the V-groove, lift the handle until the heel begins to bite, and then advance the cut. At the moment the heel begins to engage, roll the skew in a smooth, continuous motion so that the heel drops "downhill" towards the tailstock center point. Repeat the cut, until the shoulder runs in a smooth curve from the V-groove to the core of waste. Repeat the procedure at the other end of the engine cylinder—cutting the V-groove and turning down the round shoulder. When you are happy with the form, use the skew to deepen the series of divider marks.

Rerun the approach, as already described, to cut the round shoulders on the sides of the wheels. Stay away from the band at the center of each wheel—you don't want to reduce the diameter—just concentrate your efforts on matching up the shoulders.

When you are pleased with the general effect, take the skew and turn rounder shoulders on the decorative button at the tailstock end of the cylinder. This done, run straight in until the waste is reduced to a minimum. Deepen the decorative lines with V-cuts. Give the turning a swift rubdown with sandpaper, check that the chuck is good and tight, then support the workpiece in one hand—meaning the engine cylinder—and part-off with the parting tool held in the other hand (see 15–3). As you make the parting cut, ease the wood slightly away from you to avoid pinching the tool.

With the engine cylinder out of the way, tidy-up the face of the first wheel with the skew and then with sandpaper, mark in the center point, and then part-off in the way already described. Do this with both wheels.

Turning the Bucket Seat, the Trailer Wheels, and the Wheel Blocks

Take the 15-inch length of three by three inch wood, check it over for potential faults and problems, and then mount it securely on the lathe, as already described.

Start by using the gouge and the skew to turn the wood down to the largest possible diameter. Make a series of passes with the gouge to turn off the corners of

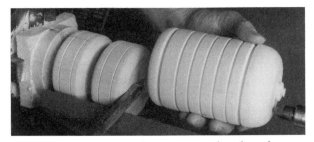

15–3   *Support the workpiece in one hand, and part-off.*

waste, and then bring the wood to a good finish with the skew. This stage accomplished, take the ruler and the divider, and set out all of the step-offs that make up the design. Working from right to left along the length of the cylinder, allow ½ inch for tailstock waste, 3 inches for the bucket seat, ¼ inch for parting waste, one inch for the first wheel, ¼ inch for waste, one inch for the second wheel, ¼ inch for waste, one inch for the third wheel, ¼ inch for waste, one inch for the fourth wheel, ¼ inch for waste, and the remainder for the two trailer axle blocks and chuck waste. Leave marking and cutting the two axle blocks until last.

With the wood clearly marked out, take the parting tool, and lower the various waste areas to a depth of about one inch so that you are left with a central core at about one inch. When you have six, clearly set out component parts—the cylinder at the headstock end for the two axles blocks, four wheel discs, and the cylinder for the bucket seat—take the gouge and the skew chisel, and turn the seat cylinder to a smaller diameter of about 2¼ inches. Take the ruler and divider, and set out all the guidelines that mark the positions of the primary V-cuts. You need step-off marks ½ inch from each end of the seat cylinder, and at the middle of each of the four wheels.

Having checked that all is correct, take the skew chisel, and turn down the round shoulders at each end of the seat cylinder. Aim for a smooth curve that runs from the decorative V-cut around to the end of the cylinder. When you are happy with the turning, sand it to a smooth finish, and part-off from the lathe.

With the seat turning off the lathe, adjust and wind in the tailstock center to pivot the first wheel in line, and set to work bringing each of the four wheels to a good finish. Use the skew chisel, or the parting tool on-edge, to make a single, decorative cut on each wheel—on the central guideline. Next, take the skew chisel and turn down the round shoulders on the edge of each wheel. Aim for a small curve of about a ⅛-inch radius—really no more than rounding off the sharp corner. Take the skew chisel, or you can use the parting tool on-edge, and run a V-cut midway between the central groove and the rounded edge.

When you have brought all four wheels to a good finish—the grooves and rounded shoulders—use a scrap of sandpaper to tidy-up the tailstock face of the first wheel in line, mark in the center point, and then part it off from the lathe. Rerun this procedure for all the wheels.

With the greater part of the turning removed, bring the tailstock center up to pivot the end of the workpiece, and mark, turn, and part-off the two 1½-inch-wide axle blocks, in much the way as already described for the wheels.

Turning the Large Tractor Wheels

Having cast your eyes over the working drawings, take one of the one-inch thick, 5½ by 5½ inch square slabs of wood, and fix the center of one side by drawing crossed diagonals. Set the divider or compass to a radius of 2½ inches, and scribe the wood with a five-inch-diameter circle. With the circle in place, run the wood swiftly through the band saw to cut away the bulk of the waste.

Mount the roughed-out blank securely on the screw chuck, and use the gouge to turn the wood to a smooth-faced, smooth-edged disc. Aim to finish up with a disc about 4¾ inches in diameter. If you are a beginner and find the square-ended gouge a bit awkward, then change over to using a scraper and/or a round-nosed gouge.

Having completed an accurately turned disc, move the tool rest over the bed of the lathe so that you can approach the workpiece face-on, and use the ruler and divider to set out the lines of the design. Working out from the center point, mark the two radius step-offs—one at ¾ inch and another at 1¾ inches. If the task is efficiently managed, the hubcap should measure 1½ inches in diameter, and the tire should measure ⅞ inches wide.

With all the guidelines in place, take the parting tool, and run a couple of ¼-inch-deep depth cuts into the wall. Next, use the tool of your choice to lower the wall of the wheel until both the hub and the tire step up and stand out in relief.

Start by working the tire. Turn down the three sharp corners so that the tire becomes more-or-less round in section. When you have worked from the high point of the face—first down towards the flat wall and then back and down towards the outside edge of the tire—then move the tool rest, change tack, and work from the back edge of the disc out-and-round towards the outermost edge of the tire.

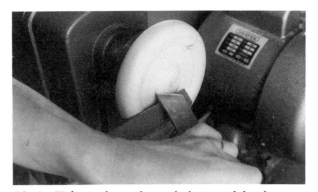

15–4 Tidy up the angles with the toe of the skew chisel so that there is a sharp step-up to the dome.

Working out from the center—with the inside curve of the gouge "looking" towards the rim—carefully turn down the sharp step to dome the hub (see 15–4). Make several right-to-left passes until the hub is a smoothly curved hump. Mark the center point with the tip of the skew chisel.

Finally, use the sandpaper to sand to a smooth finish, and then rerun for the other wheel. Be mindful that although turning a single wheel is wonderfully easy, turning a matching pair of wheels is something else again!

Turning the Tractor Wheel Guards

Study the working drawings once more (see 15–2). Take the 1¼-inch-thick slab of 6½ by 6½ inch square wood, prepare it in the manner already described—so that you have a six-inch disc—and then set to work turning it down to a dish shape. First use the gouge to turn down the curve on the outside of the bowl, and then turn down the inside. For the outside set the gouge down on what will be the high spot of the rim, and then run the gouge in a smooth, rolling action across-and-around towards the back edge of the disc to gradually turn the shape at the back of the bowl. The outside base diameter needs to be about four to 4½ inches. Having turned the outside profile, then use the gouge and the scraper to work the inside profile. Work from side to center. Enter the gouge about ½ inch in from the side edge, deepen the cut, and then run-and-roll the gouge in a smooth arc towards the center. Aim for a dish shape that fits your tractor wheel. Make repeated cuts until the overall wall thickness is about ¼ inch. Keep checking your progress with the calliper, with the wheel, and with your working drawings.

Of all the turnings that remain, the axle block with the steering rod is perhaps the most difficult, if only because it contains so many elements. You also need a couple of headlights, a washer and knob to go with the steering post, a little steering wheel, a little barrel-shaped turning for the tractor's back axle, project left-over turnings for the logs, and so on.

The Engine Block

Carefully study the project picture once more (see 15–1), the various working drawings, and your collection of turnings. Fit the sanding disc on the bowl-turning end of the lathe. Take the engine turning, decide which side is "top," and then use the sanding disc to level off the bottom and side faces. If you look at the working drawings (see 15–2), you will see that the finished engine block needs, in front view, to be about 2¼ inches wide—from flat face to flat face—and about 2⅛ inches high from the flat base to the curved top. Aim to finish up with an engine block that is more-or-less the same width as the chassis. Sand the angled face for the steering wheel, and tidy-up the decorative button at front-center. Make sure that the finished block fits fair and square on the chassis base. With the engine block held in place on the chassis—with screws—bore a ¾-inch-diameter hole from the top of the block to the underside of the chassis base. Have the hole positioned at top-center and about one inch back from the front of the chassis.

The Steering Rod

Take the steering-rod turning, and, having pencil-marked the front face of the axle-block end, sand both side faces until it measures about 1¼ inches across the flats. Next, bore a ½-inch-diameter hole through the flats—for the ½-inch-diameter axle rod. Rub the hole out with a "screw" of sandpaper so that the axle is a loose, easy fit. Push the turning in place up through the chassis and the engine block. Trim the top spigot—the

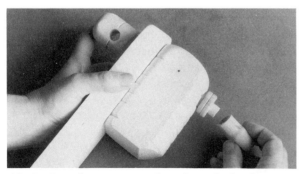

15–5   Run the steering rod up through the chassis and the engine block, and top it off with the spacer ring and the steering wheel.

step on which the spacer ring sits—so that it stands about 1⁄16 inch higher than the top of the engine block.

Drill out the spacer ring, slide it in place on top of the rod so that it butts hard up against the spigot step. Lastly, sand opposite sides of the steering knob turning, bore a ½-inch-diameter hole into its underside, and pop it in place on top of the rod (see 15–5). If all is well, there should be about a 1⁄16-inch gap between the underside of the spacer and the top of the engine block.

The Bucket Seat

Take the bucket seat turning, and bore a 1¾-inch-diameter hole straight down from the top end. Stop short about ½ inch from the bottom of the base so that you finish up with a little cylindrical pot or tub.

And now for one of the tricky bits! If you look at the working drawings and photographs, you will see that the seat shape is made by running a saw cut in a smooth curve down from the top—the pot "rim"—and out at one side. We used a coping saw, but you could just as well use a scroll saw. Bearing in mind that you only have *one shot* at getting it right, draw in a few guidelines, and then run the saw down through the pot (see page 19).

Sand the seat until the top, base, and sawn edges are smoothly rounded and contoured to the touch. This done, take the remaining small bridge-like off-cut, and press it onto the sanding disc so that it will sit level and "bridge-like" on the chassis. Rub the rounded top of the bridge down—just a smudge—so that the bucket seat can be set in place.

Lastly, not forgetting to have washers between layers, run a roundhead screw through the center of the seat, through the bridge, and into the chassis. If all is well, the bucket seat should be firmly fixed, but able to swivel.

The Tractor Wheel Guards

Take the turned dish, and set it rim-side-down on the worksurface. Run a strip of masking tape from side-to-side across the underside so that it goes in the direction of the grain, and so that one edge of the tape touches on the center of the base, marking out the midline (see 15–6, top). Fiddle around until you get it just right.

Once you are sure that all is correct, run the dish through the band saw, and, using one edge of the tape as a guide, slice it in half. Peel off the tape, set the two half-dishes together rim-to-rim—like a big sandwich—and rub down the sawn faces on the sanding disc so that they are level. Repeat this procedure with the sharp corners to cut them back at an angle. If you keep the dish rims aligned throughout this operation, you should finish up

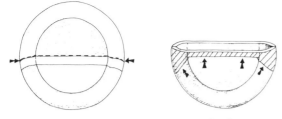

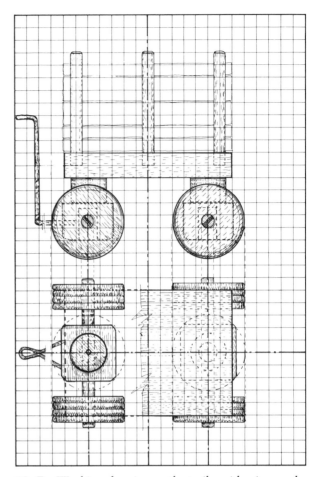

15–6 Run a strip of masking tape in the direction of the grain so that one edge marks the midway line. (Right) Being careful to keep the disc rims aligned, reduce the waste wood on the sanding disc.

with two identical wheel guards, with all edges being smooth and flush (see 15–6, right). Take a fold of sandpaper, and give the whole works a swift sanding so that all of the edges are slightly rounded. Finally, use roundhead screws to fit the guards at either side of the chassis.

The Trailer Axle Blocks

Look to the working drawings (see 15–7). Take the two 1½-inch-thick turnings—the two wheel-like discs—and use a pencil, ruler, and masking tape to run midlines around the 1½-inch thickness and across the diameter. If you've got it right, the turning should be quartered. This done, press the turnings repeatedly side-on onto the sanding disc to cut them down to squarish blocks with rounded corners. Use the drawn lines as a guide. Aim for blocks that are about 2⅛ inches across the flats.

When you have achieved the blocks, redraw the guidelines. Set the blocks dome-side up on the drill press table, and bore a ¾-inch-diameter hole through the center of the turning to a depth of about 1¼ inches. Next, bore a ½-inch-diameter hole through the side of the turning—in one flat face and out of the other—at right angle to the ¾-inch diameter holes. Sand the ½-inch hole so that the axle is an easy, smooth fit. Do this with both turnings. Bore screw holes through the center of the ¾-inch hole—on both turnings—and through the center of the little spacer turning that sits between the axle blocks and the underside of the trailer bed (see 15–8).

To fit everything in place, first screw the blocks and spacer turnings in place on the underside of the trailer bed, and then pass the axles through the block and over the head of the screw. If all is correct, there should be a slight clearance between the axles and the screw heads.

The Axles and Wheels

Start by boring ½-inch-diameter holes through the center of all eight wheels. Cut all of the axle rods to length and label them so that you don't make any mess-ups.

15–7 Working drawings—the trailer, side view and plan. The scale is two grid squares to one inch. Note that the only difference between the front and back wheel block fixing is that the front one is free to pivot, whereas the back one is clenched tight with the screw.

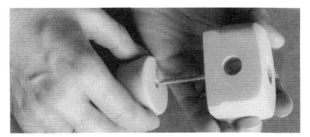

15–8 The trailer axle blocks; run the screw down through the block, through the spacer, and into the trailer bed.

The system for fitting the wheels to the axles is wonderfully simple and direct. After first sanding the middle part of the dowel—so that it is an easy-turn fit through the axle block—take a saw and, one dowel at a time, cut

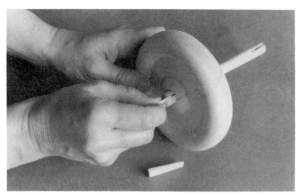

15–9 *Tap the wedge into the axle slot, until the wheel is a tight fit.*

15–11 *Detail showing how the back axle is held in place with a little, turned "bridge" block.*

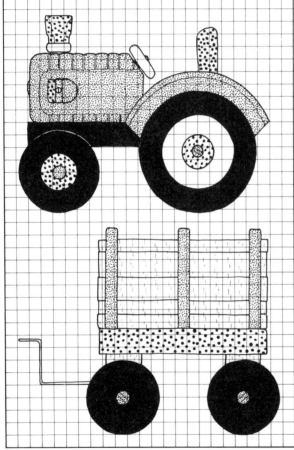

15–10 *Painting grid—the scale is two grid squares to one inch.*

a thin, wedge-shaped sliver out the end that passes through the wheel. Allow the slots to be about 1¼ inches long and no thicker than about ¹⁄₁₆ inch.

Take a piece of scrap wood and a penknife, and cut eight wedges—one for each axle end. Cut the wedges so that they are about 1½-inches long and ⅛-inch thick at the fat end. When you are ready to fit the wheels (see 15–9), all you do is slide the wheels on the dowel ends, tap the glued wedges home so that the dowel ends open up, and trim back the wedges to a good finish. Have a trial fitting of all the wheels—but hold back with the gluing and finishing until after painting (see 15–10).

Have a look at the working drawings, and see how the axle ends protrude slightly on the trailer wheels and on the large tractor wheels. Note how the tractor's front axle is located by being drilled and pegged at either side of the axle block, while the tractor's back axle is held in place by a simple "bridge" component that has been made from a barrel-like turning (see 15–11).

All the other bits and pieces—all the extra fittings— are easily made from odds and ends.

PAINTING AND FINISHING

Disassemble the toy so that you have a collection of component parts, and sit down to carefully study the painting grid (refer to 15–10). Start by painting in the main areas of ground color.

When the paint is good and dry, screw, glue, wedge, and fit everything together; sand the wheel wedges, make good any scratched paint, and give everything a couple of generous coats of varnish.

And now, at last, you have to stop playing, and give this wonderful toy over to some very lucky kid—or not!

Appendices

RECOMMENDED WOODS

Apple

A hard, dense close-grained wood—comes in small sizes, turns well, and takes a good polish. Good for small detailed toys that are going to be stained

Ash

A long-grained, tough wood—not suitable for beginners. Good for bats, handles, and such

Beech

A heavy, good-to-turn, inexpensive wood—really good for toys that need to be crisp-edged and hard-wearing—boxes, figures, dowels, and cogs

Box

A beautiful, butter-smooth hard wood with a dense even grain—really good for chessmen, small boxes, and just about any small, fine turning

Canary

(American whitewood) A yellowish soft wood, even-grained and knot-free—good for general turning. Very much like lime/basswood

Cherry

A close-grained, good-to-work red/brown wood—good for small projects. Turns well—can be brought to a high-shine finish. The American variety is known as American black cherry

Chestnut

Brown in color—it turns well

Holly

A beautiful close-grained, ivory white wood—it turns well and takes fine details. A good wood for small delicate turnings that need to be stained rather than painted.

Jelutong

A pale cream, easy-to-turn wood that can be turned, carved, and worked almost without regard to the run of the grain. If you want to make small, woodturned, painted toys at a low cost, then we recommend using jelutong—note that in North America Jelutong may be difficult to come by. We recommend any straight-grained hardwood such as linden or maple as an alternative.

Lime

(American Linden and Basswood) A close-grained, knot-free, easy-to-turn wood—the perfect wood for beginners. A bit like canary-whitewood

Maple

A dense, shiny-grained wood—traditionally used for turning

Pear

Pinkish brown in color—a good wood to turn. Traditionally used for cups, bowls, turned and carved figures, and such

Poplar

Sometimes also called American/Canadian aspen. A tough, close-textured, split-resistant wood—traditionally used for turned toys. Be warned—in the United States, canary wood and American whitewood are also sometimes called "poplar"

Pine

There are so many varieties of "pine," that the best advice is to try turning a local easy-to-find type, see how it turns, and then take it from there. For example, although pitch pine is hard and dense and very difficult to turn, once turned, the surface is beautifully smooth. And then again, parana pine—sometimes called Brazilian pine—is smooth-grained and works well

Plum

A beautiful, pink-brown wood—good to turn, with a tight grain and a hard, smooth finish. Traditionally used for small turnery—handles, bowls, and such

Sycamore

A beautiful, milk-white wood, with a close grain and a smooth, silky surface. Traditionally used for dairy/food bowls and general domestic turning—a good wood for toymaking

Walnut

Dark to light brown, a good wood for small and large turning. There are several varieties, some much better than others—have a try-out before ordering quantities. Note—if you live near a source of inexpensive wood—such as a sawmill—try a piece of local wood.

Be Warned—If you have any doubts about a wood's suitability for woodturning/toymaking—it might be toxic and it might splinter—then find out about the variety and consult a wood-supply specialist.

TIMBER FAULTS

There is no such thing as a perfect wood, or any sort of guarantee that your piece of special, expensive wood is sound and workable throughout. If you look at one or two of the projects, you will see that we started making the toy and taking the photographs, only to find that the wood had a cavity, split, knot, or some other nasty.

The best you can do, is go for a recommended wood, look out for possible problems, and then work around any flaws. There are many faults and flaws to be on the lookout for—everything from foreign bodies within the wood, hidden cavities, stains and moulds to cup shakes, dead knots, unexpected grain twists, and wet sappy areas. Before you put tool to wood, check the wood over for obvious problems, and, if you have any doubts, put it aside and go for another piece.

If by chance you are well into a project and a knot, split hollow, or whatever shows up, then either change the project to work around the problem, or settle for making the dowel/wheel/ball smaller, and then save it for another project.

Blemishes

This refers to just about anything that is uncharacteristic. One person's beautiful knots or run of grain, might well be your blemish

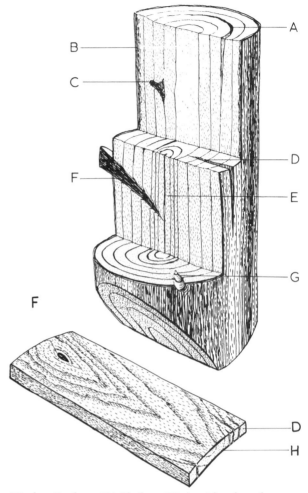

Timber Faults—(A) Shakes. (B) Avoid soft and sappy bark wood. (C) Internal fault—difficult to spot. (D) Split caused by rapid drying. (E) Heartwood can be very dense and difficult to turn. (F) Avoid dead or loose knots. (G) A knot that has fallen away will leave a scar or hole. (H) Planks warp or bend in the opposite way to the run of the grain.

Checks

A check is a split or crack in the length of the plank/ board/section—a split runs down the length of the grain. Since the check is an indicator of possible larger problems, it is best to look for another piece of wood

Decay

If the wood is soft, spongy or crumbly, or it looks to be affected with worm holes, fungus or white stains, then the chances are the wood is starting to decay. If this is the case, then put it to one side and look for another piece.

Knots

Knots are termed dead, hollow, loose, spiked, encased, and so on. Knots are difficult to turn, so it is best to avoid them if possible

Shakes and Splits

Separations that occur throughout the length of a log are termed "shakes" and "splits." If, when you look at a log or plank end-on, you see a heart-shaped crack in the middle of the wood, or star-shaped cracks around the edge of the wood, then the chances are there might be hollows, cracks, and splits within the wood. Since there is nothing quite so disheartening, as going to all the trouble of mounting the wood on the lathe, turning it and all the rest, only to find out that the wood contains a split or crack, it pays to spend time looking the wood over for possible problems

Metric Conversion

Inches to Millimetres and Centimetres						
MM—*millimetres*			CM—*centimetres*			
Inches	MM	CM	Inches	CM	Inches	CM
⅛	3	0.3	9	22.9	30	76.2
¼	6	0.6	10	25.4	31	78.7
⅜	10	1.0	11	27.9	32	81.3
½	13	1.3	12	30.5	33	83.8
⅝	16	1.6	13	33.0	34	86.4
¾	19	1.9	14	35.6	35	88.9
⅞	22	2.2	15	38.1	36	91.4
1	25	2.5	16	40.6	37	94.0
1¼	32	3.2	17	43.2	38	96.5
1½	38	3.8	18	45.7	39	99.1
1¾	44	4.4	19	48.3	40	101.6
2	51	5.1	20	50.8	41	104.1
2½	64	6.4	21	53.3	42	106.7
3	76	7.6	22	55.9	43	109.2
3½	89	8.9	23	58.4	44	111.8
4	102	10.2	24	61.0	45	114.3
4½	114	11.4	25	63.5	46	116.8
5	127	12.7	26	66.0	47	119.4
6	152	15.2	27	68.6	48	121.9
7	178	17.8	28	71.1	49	124.5
8	203	20.3	29	73.7	50	127.0

Inches ——

Millimetres ——

Centimetres ——

Index